Emotional Harmony

Using SomEx^{SM} – A Somatic Experiential
Intervention to Repair and Transform Your Life

KENT D. FISHER

With

MICHELLE RAPPAPORT

BALBOA.
PRESS
A DIVISION OF HAY HOUSE

Balboa Press books may be ordered through booksellers or by contacting:

Balboa Press
A Division of Hay House
1663 Liberty Drive
Bloomington, IN 47403
www.balboapress.com
1 (877) 407-4847

Print information available on the last page.

ISBN: 978-1-5043-4230-8 (sc)
ISBN: 978-1-5043-4231-5 (e)

Library of Congress Control Number: 2015916329

Balboa Press rev. date: 11/30/2015

Contents

Jazz Prayer

by Vanessa Rush Southern

God of syncopated rhythms and dissonant riffs.

God of lone saxophone solos
On a summer's night
On a steamy subway platform

God who brings chord progressions into resolution
Or who keeps two themes in creative tension forever

God who brings music from any instrument
From a straight woman in grief
From gay women in love
From a man born in a woman's body
Or a woman born in a man's
From those who choose to live alone

No matter what we are in this life
Who we were born and who we hope to become
No matter what shape our bodies, what politics
What sex or what gender What education
No matter what

O God, make us instruments of thy will
Sowing love, making love, making music, too.

Improvisation
Accompaniment
Call and Response
Theme and variation
Ebb and flow
You and Me

Music
Moving with the Spirit
Pure Jazz

May our lives, O God, be Pure Jazz!
Amen
from This Piece of Eden

Acknowledgements

I want to begin by expressing my appreciation to my friend and colleague Tennie McCarty for encouraging me to share my work with others by writing this book. She has been a mentor and an inspiration for me in doing this powerful work to put my 25 years of practice into a methodology that can be taught and integrated for other practitioners. Tennie is one of a few pioneers in the field of recovery and trauma work that I am so grateful for the path that has been laid before me.

Without my business partner and friend Michelle Rappaport, none of this would have come to fruition. She has been a mighty companion these many years in creating this work and supporting countless individuals on the road of recovery. As she talks about in the book, her personal journey in dealing with chronic illness continues to be a source of awe for me to see the grace with which she masters her life. She is my hero.

I want to thank Kristen McGuiness for the work she did in developing and assisting on this book project. It was her expertise and perseverance that made this possible.

A word about the precious individuals who come to us for repair and healing; humbling. I am so honored and hold in reverence the resilient people that come to do this work and find the courage to transform their lives. I hold sacred the trust with which they put into this process. I appreciate the clients that were willing to share part of their story for this book and their desire to provide a resource to others suffering.

Specifically I want to thank "Cathy" for her courage to tell her story and for the willingness to share it not only with the group of people she came to know as her recovery community but for others to hear and hopefully find hope in the resilience that helps us to transform our live.

Lastly, to my precious boys, Jamie and Jordan, this book is dedicated to you. It is for you that I find the passion to do, teach and share this work. I have dreamed of having children since I was old enough to dream. Due to my own shortcomings I am not always the parent I want to be. It is in this work of emotional regulation that I strive to be a safe, sober father for you to lean into. May everything I do benefit your highest good and that of all the children, small or grown, that deserve a place to grow into their divine selves. I am honored to be your father.

Introduction

L ife is messy. Whatever your life story might entail, nobody's is simple. It is filled with tragedies and traumas, heartbreak and disappointment. But healing and recovery are possible. No matter how difficult or painful your circumstances, there exist today vast possibilities to help us find a path towards transforming our lives. As people enter our offices unaware of their resilience and the potential for change, we offer them this path towards recovering their Authentic Self.

I know when I first landed on that therapist's couch, I wouldn't have stayed very long if I had not known it was possible for me to heal. It is what the great psychiatrist Victor Frankl deemed, "the last of the human freedoms"—the ability to "choose one's attitude in a given set of circumstances." Unfortunately, most of us don't have the life tools to consciously choose the path our life takes. Instead, we have learned to adapt to the world around us, molding our identity to fit the roles we have been asked to play. We develop relationships to people, places, and things, believing they might help to balance our emotional states. We create adaptable selves to protect our deeper vulnerabilities, to adjust to whatever messiness life has thrown our way, and we lose our Authentic Self in the process—falling into codependency, addiction, and the false beliefs about who we are and what our potentials might be because we were never allowed to engage that potential in the first place. But belonging is a basic need for all of us, often prompting us to compromise our boundaries and even our core identity in order to feel a sense of connection. And then we end up on that therapist's couch wondering why the choices we have made for ourselves have left us lost and isolated, victimized and alone.

Almost twenty years ago, my business partner Michelle Rappaport and I opened our therapeutic practice in Memphis, Tennessee. We founded the Experiential Healing Center to help people start finding repair and harmony in their life where before there was only discord. We operate from the belief that nobody has a child with the intention of screwing him or her up. For most people raising children (and for most people in general), they're simply doing the best they can with what they know until they know something different. And for most families, these patterns of behaviors stretch far into the family genogram. It is handed down generation after generation until finally one member stands up and says, "No more. I want a different life."

There is a place in everyone where we can achieve Emotional Harmony. In clinical terms that place is known as the "Optimal Arousal Zone." This book will help you discover and explore that innate place in yourself in order to recover the parts that had to be compartmentalized in order to survive. Unaware of how to be our own choice makers, we lose the pieces of ourselves that make up a whole and healthy human: physical health, emotional wellbeing, social relationships, mental health, spirituality, and our own free will.

Twenty-five years ago, I had all but lost this personal identity. I grew up feeling fearful and anxious in a small town in West Virginia. My mother had already had four children and was in the middle of her pregnancy with me when my alcoholic father announced he was leaving her for another woman. From the moment she learned she was pregnant, I believe my mother was overwhelmed by her circumstances, and as I grew up, I could feel that. Though being called sensitive might have bothered me as a child, I can't tell you how grateful I am for this quality today. But back then the one person I was most sensitive to, and the primary source of my trauma bonding, was my mother.

As a young child, I felt the need to take care of my mother, believing that I could be her source of joy just as much as I believed I was her source of pain. Though I received affection from my sisters, I could never seem to get the approval and acceptance from my mother that I thought would heal that longing in my soul.

For Michelle, her childhood was similarly shaped by another wounded and depressed mother. By the time she was fourteen, she had shaved half of her head and discovered that she could self-soothe with food. Though her mother was "dedicated" to raising her children, whereas my mother spent more of her time at church, we both walked away unsure of how to participate in relationships or how to develop healthy boundaries.

Thankfully, for me, I found music. I played the trumpet in band, and I loved it. I loved hearing the notes of my instrument as it joined in with the other sections, melding into the symphonic experience of the group. Band was my solace from not feeling a sense of belonging at home. My older siblings were long out of the house, and my mother was by that time remarried. I had already discovered alcohol and drugs, which gave me a temporary reprieve from dealing with the secret that I believed no one could know—the secret of who I really was, which at that time, was a secret even to me. I was a young gay man with no healthy modeling about what that meant.

But standing there amongst my peers, playing music, I found a connection between others and myself. There was a trust there between us that when we all played we would find congruity in chaos. We would find harmony. I decided I wanted to become a music minister. I thought that music could save me from the world and that religion might be able to save me from myself.

Instead, addiction took both from me.

For seven years, until I turned 24, I did not take a sober breath. I believed that there was no point in owning more than what I could fit in my car. I figured if I were always moving, I wouldn't have to stop long enough to see myself in the mirror. I wouldn't have to see that defeated young man who had stopped allowing himself to love. I just sought escape with more alcohol and drugs and sex to erase the identity I was so terrified to embrace. Then, one afternoon I found myself on that bridge. You know that bridge. That one where you look down at the river and think, "Maybe that's the easier way. Maybe life is simply too painful, too unbearable, too messy to keep living." But then something inside me said, "No, not yet."

Like Dr. Frankl describes in *Man's Search for Meaning*, our survival is contingent on this idea that life is still expecting something from us. And though I believed at that time it would be better to be dead than gay, some glimmer in me knew my journey could help others. Dr. Frankl found that many of the survivors during the Holocaust found the strength to survive based on the belief that one day they would be needed. And something in me, some quiet whisper from my Authentic Self, told me I would be.

By the age of twenty-four I was homeless, living in my car, fired from almost every job I had yet to hold, and lacking anything even close to a sense of self-identity, and still I believed I might yet have something to contribute. I ended up in treatment instead of at the bottom of that river, and though I might have had a DUI and an attitude when I first came into recovery, I also had the primary commitment that I was going to tell the truth. After working through the substance abuse that had become my smokescreen for who I was, I had to face the core issues lying underneath, the number one offender and the number one reason why people relapse or use in the first place: my relationship with others and myself.

When folks come to the Experiential Healing Center, we explain that at the foundation of most unhealthy patterns or habits is what we would call disordered attachment. It is in these unhealthy attachments that we create that Adaptable Self that lives outside our Optimal Arousal Zone. When we are living outside this zone, we are either in the depression of collapse or the intensity of activation, which are our two primary means of experiencing relationships. In that space, we seldom experience emotional harmony. It is in this ability to adapt to the relational and environmental influences around us that we form and build unhealthy relationships with other people, substances and/or processes. In turn, we create relational and sexual templates that guide the trajectory of our lived experience. When life stressors cause us to live either overly anxious and agitated, or overwhelmed and disconnected, we will seek ways to self soothe this discomfort, often through those same templates, believing they provide relief when really they only deepen the burden.

And my client Cathy was no different.

When I met Cathy she had four kids, a terrible second marriage, and was living off the last remnants of what had once been a sizable inheritance. Upon our first meeting, Cathy quickly explained that she wanted to fix herself and reclaim her husband. But it wasn't the first time she had done that. Cathy had lived for over twenty years in a sexually abusive relationship with her first husband, and the father of her children. Throughout the course of that marriage, Cathy's husband Bill had had sex with her whenever he wanted. Whether she was sick, pregnant, tired, and, often, even when she said no. And then when Cathy managed to get up some gumption and started placing locks on the doors, her husband began to look elsewhere, taking up mistresses in her absence. Finally, he left her for his final affair. Though heart broken, it didn't take long before Cathy had found someone else. She had married yet another sex addict, Chris, who she had recently found out was also having an affair.

Having learned from her first marriage, that affairs eventually end in divorce, Cathy had become obsessed with saving the marriage. A devout Baptist, she didn't believe in divorce and was terrified to find herself in its clutches again. She needed a man to feel safe even though the men she chose always seemed to threaten her security.

She had never learned nor had ever been taught how to be her own choice maker. She appeared disassociated from herself and others. She has never had the physical, emotional, or spiritual freedom to make healthy boundaries and choices for herself.

When I first went into the psychology field, I decided I wanted to work with foster children, and though my work took me in a very different direction, to a certain extent I still do work with children: they're just in grown up bodies. When Michelle and I founded EHC, we began in the experiential method. We later incorporated the somatic therapies that have transformed the field of psychotherapy today, applying a variety of techniques to the therapeutic process, using experiential methods to help folks oscillate within their Optimal Arousal Zone in order to skirt the edges of their activation and collapse.

Together, we began to see that both schools of thought were not only mutually supportive, but also practically seamless in their execution. These therapies are action-oriented modalities that are designed to help access feelings and develop choice making about how we react and repair when life pulls us out of our Optimal Arousal Zones. We don't wound alone, and we certainly don't heal alone. SomEx[SM] is a Somatic Experiential intervention to treat trauma and addiction. SomEx[SM] honors this process, connecting the left-brain hemisphere of rationalization, reasoning, and meaning making to the right hemisphere's ability for social engagement and emotional processing.

By incorporating Dan Siegel's five strategies for the brain and Sharon Stanley's somatic transformation work with our own understanding of these therapies – we began to see that SomEx[SM] worked in five simple parts:

- Somatic Attention – By becoming aware of our body's story, we are able to integrate the cognitive, left-brain narrative of our life story with its emotional, body-based effects. Through SomEx[SM], these effects become amplified in the initial stages of the therapeutic process wherein the therapist is able to call the client's attention to their motions, movements, breath, and other reactions.

- Somatic Trust – In working with a trained therapist, people are able to experience a healthy attachment to someone who can help them define boundaries and identify needs. This therapeutic approach necessitates the need for the therapist to have attunement to his or her own Optimal Arousal Zone.

- Somatic Modification – Through the process of somatic inquiry, the therapist is able to help the client oscillate between a regulated state and the edges of their Optimal Arousal Zone, strengthening their ability to react and repair in stressful environments. Through psychodrama, props, art therapy, and other processes that help access the right-hemisphere, we can re-negotiate and repair the behavioral patterns around disordered attachments and traumatic events.

- Somatic Intervention – Through this strengthened resiliency, people are able to unlearn the fixed action patterns of their childhood and family belief systems, and begin to re-negotiate their emotional responses to life's circumstances. SomEx^{SM} allows for a meaningful and interactive dialogue between caregivers and clients, which helps to expand empathy and awareness around how their belief systems have impaired emotional harmony in their family systems for generations.

- Somatic Practice –SomEx^{SM} is a deep, integrative process, which requires an ongoing commitment to the work. Much like the Twelve Steps maxim to "practice these principles in all areas of our lives," emotional regulation and harmony must be taken out of the therapist's office and into the world around us.

By repairing the disorganized and insecure attachments of our childhood through somatic engagement, and by building resiliency through the use of experiential therapies such as psychodrama, art therapy, role-playing, and play therapy, we are able to connect with the thwarted emotions of our childhood, and rediscover that self that lives within all of us - playful, passionate, unashamed, unafraid, eager to learn and grow.

At EHC, we believe this is the difference between therapy and counseling. Therapy is a co-regulated process where therapist and client embark on a journey to recover and repair the Authentic Self. Many clients engage in the comprehensive work of reconstructing their lives and selves while some choose to celebrate this work publicly in what we call a Reconstruction Day. The reconstruction process involves bringing together all the individual notes that frame a person's life and integrating them into an orchestrated harmony that helps them find the song within themselves. This is a cautious, integrated, restorative process that allows for the transformation from "stuckness" to authenticity. In many ways, the Reconstructions are my way back into being a music minister because for the person who is having the reconstruction process I act, to an extent, as their conductor, weaving together the pieces of their life.

As our therapeutic relationship deepened, Cathy chose to participate in a Reconstruction Day. Through the work (both before, during, and after), Cathy was able to integrate those left-brain rationalizations she had been telling herself her whole life with the emotional memory that had been frozen in her right-hemisphere since childhood. This is what is at the core of the somatic work we do, engaging that part of us that experienced the trauma first hand, the parts of our brain that store not just the narrative memory but the cellular memory as well. By integrating these separate parts, we are able to move from the compartmentalized discord of our adaptable selves into the true symphony of our Authentic Self.

This is not work that can be done at home nor alone. As a member of twelve-step programs, I quickly realized the healing properties of the group. But long before that, there were the healing properties of the tribe. And if we search back long and hard enough in our genealogy, we all come from a tribe. In this community, we learn from others' experiences and strength that we are not alone. Now, as you begin to go through this work, it's important that you begin seeking a healing community that resonates with your experience. If you are currently active in an addiction, you can't do this level of repair. We need to heal from the symptoms before we can treat the source of the disease. *We do not wound alone, and we do not heal alone.* The tribe honors this healing, it celebrates it, and in that celebration, we connect back into the deepest parts of ourselves, the parts that live in emotional harmony, determined not just to survive, but to embrace "the last of the human freedoms"—the ability to "choose one's attitude in a given set of circumstances."

PART ONE

Attachment

CHAPTER ONE

Emotionally Disregulated Families

I have a good friend, Tennie McCarty, who always says, "If it's hysterical, it's historical." The truth is, for most of us, we still behave out of a set of fixed action patterns, passed down from generations and then developed and established throughout childhood. These fixed action patterns are automatic, unconscious responses to the world around us, some of which are healthy or benign behaviors we do everyday. Others can be embedded responses to frozen or held traumatic memory, which evolve into habituated behavioral patterns that displace us from our Optimal Arousal Zone. We think we are our own choice makers, but we don't realize how often our experiences of activation or collapse are actually rooted in past relational templates and family system patterns established well before our own births.

When Cathy graduated high school, she decided she would join her cousins, who were working and living on their family farm in east Texas. For Cathy, that farm had always been a great source of reprieve from the violence and fear that consumed her childhood home. She wanted to go to college, but then, in her senior year, her father passed away. The source of so much of that violence, Cathy wasn't sure how to manage her emotions. In addition, her father's death brought an unexpected weight: an inheritance that Cathy never imagined would be hers so soon.

3

With money on the table and a family business looking for its new head, Cathy decided to run. And so to the old family farm she went, but her memories weren't far behind. As she later told me:

> In many ways, it was like my father was there waiting for me. My first night, I remembered back to one of our trips there when I was eight. For most of the day, we were allowed to run and play, which was such a release from the confines of our home in Dallas. But then that first night, I am standing in our dining room, staring at the table, remembering how my dad's moods could change even at the ranch, and it comes back to me. Mom is cooking in the kitchen. All of us kids are in the dining room. Everyone is seated around the table except me. I am standing between the window and the pantry door. Someone starts chanting, "We wanna eat. We wanna eat." The rest of the kids at the table join in. They pick up their silverware and clomp the ends on the table in rhythm with the chant. "We wanna eat! We wanna eat!" Dad comes down the hall, and I jump to my seat so as not be caught being up from the table. He strides into the room and goes around the table slamming our heads together, two by two as everyone begins to cry.
>
> He yells at us. Jacki says, "Cathy wasn't doing it." He looks at me and raises his eyebrow. I looked down at my lap.

This was the fear and threat of violence in which Cathy was raised. According to Sharon Stanley, leading scholar-practitioner in the field of somatic psychotherapy, "In many cultures people recognize that survival depends on a network of relationships with self, neighbor, land, ancestors, traditional practices, animals, and the universe." And, certainly in our culture, this network is centered in and around the family. It is through social engagement with our primary caregivers and siblings that we are able to connect to ourselves and to others. Now, in my own home growing up, we did not have such an aggressor. Though my father's rage wasn't present, it was still felt, lending to a similarly debilitating lesson in emotional regulation: silence. In Michelle's house, you had to shout to even be heard. But for all of us and the generations of emotionally dis-regulated families in our culture today, we all share one common bond: fear. This fear can take on a million forms—whether through the violence of one member or, as in my home, the silence of another. Fear is often passed down without saying a word.

And then we grow up, thinking we have outrun our past, only to realize we are repeating those same patterns of fear and silence, violence and anger that we watched take over the households of our childhood. As Ken Adam's explains in his seminal work, *Silently Seduced*, "The family system works to seek balance and tries to correct itself even in adulthood. As long as the abuse or neglect experienced in childhood remains buried within, we recreate our family all over again in adult relationships."

Again, it is often not the fault of any one family member that this way of relating to each other and the outside world takes place. People do the best they can with what they've got, but for most of our families, they were raised in similar homes with similar rules and systems, and often, similar non-existent boundaries. Sick families beget sick families until someone wakes up one day and says, "No more."

For Cathy, that day came three years into her second marriage, after four children and her new husband's first affair. She was tired. Tired of thinking she was buying a new set of goods only to find they were as defective as the ones before. Chris had started out as such a loving breath of fresh air. He wanted her to go back to school, he loved her children as if they were his own, and he expressed compassion and frustration at her years of sexual abuse with Bill, but then she found the email account. The one she didn't know existed. Soon after she found the emails between him and a woman in Chicago, where he had been going for work. She was tired of feeling that sinking feeling in her gut, the doubt and betrayal that only a lover can exact.

Though Cathy had wanted to find someone who would treat her right, she had been groomed her whole life to be attached to how the external picture *looked* rather than how the internal reality *felt*. Growing up in a wealthy Baptist home in Dallas, her parents presented the most wholesome of pictures. The fact that her father drank, that he terrorized the children, that he cheated on their mother, was all erased when they went to Church on Sundays and shook hands with the other congregants. When a child doesn't have security at home, their first coping skill becomes fantasy. Cathy can still remember kissing her stuffed animals, pretending they were handsome princes come to take her to faraway lands.

As children, our clients often developed filtering systems that normalized untrustworthy messages, developing bonds of trust with people who were shaming, degrading, and/or exploitive. Into adulthood, they then find themselves attracted to the same qualities that once threatened them. They are oriented to the fixed action patterns associated with their past traumas and are unable to properly discern danger in the present moment. As Ken Adams explains, "This is an effort to work out and resolve that childhood pain. Yes, the family system continues to affect one's life even when one is no longer living at home and has dismissed childhood as gone and best forgotten."

Emotionally dis-regulated families try to hold themselves together through a combination of guilt and pity, which they call "love," establishing the emotional enmeshment and avoidance that constitutes love addiction. They are consistently chasing the fantasy of what love can bring, and then backing away from the reality of what love gives. Unfortunately, in the dis-regulated family system, they have been taught that intensity, criticism, fantasy, and secrets are all synonymous with unconditional love.

This is our starting point. This is where we begin. This is when the mind is forming and being imprinted with the fixed action patterns of our behaviors and mimicking the reactions of the world around us, either validating the behaviors we see or rejecting them. In my home, silence and depression reigned, yet from an early age, I responded by acting out. I screamed and threw tantrums, breaking the silence of our household in the only way my young mind knew how.

For Cathy, violence ruled, yet she responded with a silent and saddened compliance. She did not scream; she cried. From an early age, she felt like she wanted her eyes to be closed all the time. She was ready to crawl into the bed of her depression and never wake up.

At birth, our brains are rich with neurons. We come to this world with a pulsing mass of neurological fibers ready to translate and communicate to the world around us, but those neurons have yet to be connected. It is through experience that we begin to build that connective network that ultimately forms the human mind. When we experience neglect and trauma in early childhood, the growth of that network is inhibited.

If a distressed infant is not soothed by his or her caregiver, it will respond with innate expressions, appealing to be validated and soothed. As Stephen Porges writes, the child experiences a "sudden and rapid transition from an unsuccessful strategy of struggling requiring massive sympathetic activation to the metabolically conservative immobilized state mimicking death." The body, brain, and nervous system hits a level of activation that is simply too high, flipping the switch in the child's system to a state of collapse and despair. When a parent is not attuned to the child and its needs, brain connectivity fails to develop at a healthy and natural pace, making the child "vulnerable to future developmental shock and trauma," according to Porges.

For many adults, this same pattern is re-enacted, moving between the fight, flight, or freeze states by participating in self-soothing addictions or being affected by mood disorders such as depression. We become so wired to these impaired states outside of our arousal zone that we remain trapped in the activation, or as Cathy learned to do, we dissociate altogether. Often we learn to do both.

"The addict is coming!"

Cathy told me a story of how her children once reacted to a weekend visit from their father.

> *Bill had called and said that he could come and visit the kids on a Saturday for their soccer games. The morning of the games, he called and asked directions to the field. When I got off the phone, I said, 'That was your dad. He is in town and coming to your games.'*
>
> *Up until that point we had had a pretty relaxing morning. We'd been up for a couple of hours, and the kids had gathered all their gear the night before. We had about an hour before we needed to leave, and were all in various stages of readiness. Almost immediately after the phone call, the energy in the house changed. The kids started running around looking for their stuff as it hid in plain sight. My son Ryan who was 12 at the time asked me every three minutes when we were leaving, and when I took a phone call about fifteen minutes before, he lurked in my doorway, looking at an imaginary watch and pleading with his eyes for me to get off the phone. On the way, he kept asking how fast I was going and what the speed limit was. I was able to observe all of this because, for once, I was not acting the same way. It*

> *was like everyone was running around, hollering, "The*
> *addict is coming! The addict is coming!"*

For many of us, we spend our whole lives in this hyper vigilant state of alert. For me, my mother's woundedness was a constant presence in our house. When I was a small child, my mother and I shared a room, sleeping in bunk beds. Though we did not share a bed, we might as well have because the emotional caretaking between us had begun. I could sense the pain and neglect she felt by my father's abandonment, leaving her for another woman when she was still pregnant with me, and I felt that she was now my responsibility to soothe and comfort. This was the relational template I have carried throughout my life— caretaking people who looked for me to soothe and comfort their own woundedness.

According to Pia Mellody, in her book *Facing Love Addiction*, there are stages to this process. For many of us, we often can't see this love addiction because it has been modeled in those emotionally dis-regulated family relationships since childhood. We believe the addiction dance between mother and child, father and child, and partner and partner are all perfectly normal. And we have been trained by the family system to believe as much.

As Mellody explains, love addiction begins with increasing tolerance of inappropriate behavior from others. When Cathy was eight years old, she was molested by an older neighbor. The man had already sexually abused two of her sisters, but then came after Cathy, touching her genitals and laughing at her response. After the experience, her sisters finally told their parents what was happening at the neighbor's house. Whether out of fear, ignorance, or neglect, Cathy's parents failed to do much about it other than to tell the children not to go there anymore. The neighbor was never charged with his behaviors, later confronting Cathy on the street about it, asking if her parents had stopped her and her siblings from coming to his house. By the time Cathy made it to adulthood, she had little understanding about how sexual relations should be conducted.

When her husband told her that women were supposed to consent to their husband's sexual demands, she believed him. He told her that because of her molestation, she didn't understand what was normal and what was not. Since, after Cathy's molestation, no word was ever mentioned about it—there was no healing, no counseling, no repair—to a certain extent, Bill was right: she didn't know what was normal and what was not. And for many years, she believed Bill's abuse was actually commonplace for marriage.

As Patrick Carnes explains in his work on trauma and abuse, *The Trauma Bond*, "Most people can have an emergency, respond well, and return to normal. But when the trauma is overwhelming and/or sustained, the body's ability to stay in an alarm state becomes enhanced. The alarm state starts to feel normal." For Cathy, sexual abuse became her "normal." She had never learned to create healthy sexual boundaries. Instead, she had formed her sexual identity out of fantasy and abuse, and then, when she met someone who exhibited the same definition of "normal," she suffered for years in silence, increasing her tolerance to her husband's ever-demanding and demeaning sexual behaviors.

Pia Mellody explains that there is a second step in the progress of love addiction: dependence on the person. According to Mellody, "love addicts surrender more and more of their responsibility for daily tasks of the relationship to the other party." For Cathy, this happened financially from the beginning. After she returned to the family farm, Cathy found herself paralyzed by the financial responsibility she had recently inherited. Though the family lived and socialized in an upper middle class world, she had never known that there was a small family fortune being amassed behind it. And, suddenly, there she was: eighteen, terrified, and with a bank account that she had been given full claim to, though she did little with it.

When she met Bill in her third month in East Texas, he seemed like the solution. From a hard-working background, he spoke about his big plans for investing money in the lumber industry, which was booming alongside the Texas real estate market. He seemed to only need a little seed money in order to make his fortune grand. Cathy quickly found herself buying into his dreams, believing she had found the answer to her prayers: a strong yet gentle man who played his guitar at night and lacked the authority of the father with which she had been raised. When Bill asked for her hand in marriage after only six weeks, she said, "Yes," looking forward to the life they were about to build with her money and his ambition.

At first, there was a sense of freedom once it was handed over to someone else. She told me, "At first I felt free, but now looking back, I realized that I was handing over my power, not my burden." Cathy quickly allowed Bill to make all the decisions for the family business. He was the one to decide who was hired and who was fired, and when he decided to use the profits to open up a small local newspaper so he could have his own column and could gain the recognition he had similarly sought in the Church, Cathy stood by and watched her family money being dumped into a venture that wasn't profitable a single day of its existence.

The third step in this addiction is a decrease in self-care. I remember the day Cathy stepped into my office. I wish I could say I don't see this all the time, but she had clearly stopped caring for herself long before. She wore no makeup, her hair was disheveled, and she seemed to be wearing clothes she had bought nearly a decade before. Though she once had the money to shop at the finest stores and was married to Chris, who was financially stable, she dressed and acted like a woman thirty years older than her age. She was so late, she almost missed the appointment, and I wondered just how many times in her life she had missed out on opportunities for herself.

Cathy had long ago given up on Cathy. Everything about her relationships with Chris and Bill told her she was not enough. The way Chris cheated on her, knowing everything she had already been through. The way Bill had sexually abused her for years, and then left her for another woman. And she stood by in both relationships, allowing the traumas to continue yet determined to save the relationships in which those traumas were occurring. We should all have a choice around how we move in and out of relationships and the behaviors in which we want to participate. When we have attachments that are supportive and nurturing and coherent, we are able to see our own identity and value. But when we are mired in relational templates that demand we adapt to behaviors that should be considered unacceptable, we begin to separate our Authentic Selves from the outside world. Cathy was so removed from any kind of social engagement, she not only didn't know who she was, she didn't believe she was worth much either.

The fourth stage of this addictive process is a numbing of feelings. For many, this numbness has been a part of their lives long before the actual love partner shows up. It is just a form of the dissociation they have lived in since childhood. As Cathy later explained, "When I went to treatment [for codependency] for the first time, I kept feeling nauseated. Finally, one of the counselors explained that she had experienced the same thing when she started recovery. She told me I was feeling nauseas, because I was finally having feelings."

For Cathy, she had long disassociated from her trauma-filled childhood. She had become numb to her father's violence, her mother's depression, the molestation that happened when she was eight, and the fear that permeated her entire life. She was so removed from her body, it wasn't until she was two years into her therapeutic work that she began to connect back into her body, learning to stay present in her own skin.

The fifth stage, according to Mellody is "an overpowering sense of being stymied and helpless to fix the relationship, or to escape the pain by ending it." Once it was discovered that Chris was keeping a girlfriend, Cathy tried to kick him it out, but over the course of the next year, she allowed Chris to move back in many times. Every time he would come back, there would be a brief honeymoon period filled with lots of sex and promises, but at the first hint of trouble, he would run back to Mary, his mistress. Cathy was lost in the cycle of love addiction. She knew where it was going to end, yet she was willing to accept the outcome.

In Cathy's faith, marriage is a sacred vow. It is a sacrament, an act of Christ himself, and though many in her faith and her church went through divorces, Cathy being one of them, she was raised to believe that you stood by your man. That marriage was a lifelong vow, and had Bill not left, she would have probably still been with him. Her faith provided the music to the addictive dance, giving her what she believed was good reason to accept unacceptable behaviors.

She isn't the first person I have seen to be trapped by their religion. Unfortunately, I think a lot of people are religiously abused—and I use that term when religion is used to constrict people's ability to express themselves. If religion is used to shame, guilt, and oppress versus affirm, support, and nurture, it is part of an abusive system. For Cathy, she had spent years going to her minster asking for help with her husband, but despite many well-intentioned counseling sessions, the best they could really offer her was to "just keep trying."

In the final stages of love addiction, the addict becomes incapable of seeing any of the good in the relationship even where there might be some. They become the abuser – angry, selfish, filled with resentment. They strike out at their partner. For Cathy, her focus was attached to the other woman, Mary. She was relentless in her attacks on a woman she had never met.

She harassed Chris consistently as to whether he was with her and later, after she had moved out of their home and had come to Tennessee, she continued to check emails and voicemails to see when and how often Chris and Mary were seeing one other.

As she told me, "I couldn't speak to him without screaming at him. It was as if my anger was a boiling rage, and there was nothing I could do to control it."

Caught between withdrawal and retaliation, Cathy was on a sinking ship, and then she came to a calm, quiet thud in my office—alone, bewildered, and finally ready for change.

"Distant but cordial"

But how does this addiction form? Why do some of us find ourselves engaged in the dance of love addiction and love avoidance? The love addict is someone who becomes addicted to the avoidant. They feel that if only they had the avoidant's full love and attention, they would be okay. They would be healed. The avoidant refuses to give such love but also refuses to leave the relationship. Often they act out through sexual addiction or affairs, avoiding committed intimacy through fleeting intimacy. This only engenders more need on the part of the addict, deepening their dependency and their willingness to accept increasingly neglectful behavior. The cycle continues where the love avoidant pushes the addict away until the addict breaks and tries to assert some control. The avoidant then comes back, begging for forgiveness and their "rightful" place in the relationship structure. This can take place between a parent and a child, romantic partners, siblings, co-workers, friends, and any number of human relationships. And the one thing that both of these partners share in this dance is a mutual codependency.

Codependency. We've all heard the word by now—probably too many times—but it's at the root of almost everyone's addiction.

Co-dependency is a stunted identity development created by our family of origin and our culture, resulting in the overemphasis of things on the outside of us and an under-emphasis of things on the inside of us. From this, we begin to rely more on external people, places, and things, and we minimize or deny the things on the inside, such as boundaries, feelings, wants, needs, and dreams. This split can impair relationships, affecting our physical health and emotional well being, but, perhaps most distinctly, it leads us to believe that by adapting and pleasing the people around us, our internal needs will be magically met. Codependency lives and grows in this lie.

A family's function should be to meet the needs of the children and to teach them how to meet their own needs. If these needs are being met, those children will grow up to be healthy and fulfilled as a result of the family system, not codependent and self-medicating as a consequence of its dysfunctionality. Some of the most toxic families are where the child is supposed to meet the adult's needs.

By the age of fourteen, Cathy was illegally driving her mother's car to the grocery store to do the family shopping, and then cook for her six brothers and sisters almost nightly when she came home from school.

Michelle often shares that when she and her husband first decided to have children, they thought it would be fun, and then their first son came home and she quickly found out that he demanded more of her time than she ever thought she could give another human being. But she also found out she could do it. She could give him the love and attention and care that he needed to be okay in this world. Similarly, I work everyday to keep my sons physically and psychologically safe while at the same time giving them the space and freedom to make mistakes and grow. It is our job to provide our children with boundaries, but within a space they can fall down in, where they can make mistakes, where they can be young boys growing up in this messy world with us there to guide them.

Sadly for Cathy, there was no one there to protect or guide her. She became her younger siblings' protector, and she quickly began to take on her mother's pain. There were no boundaries. Her father was physically violent from her first memories and was consistently cheating on her mother. The children were taught that the parent was always right, and if that was true, then violence and dishonesty were also right. Being untrustworthy was normal, getting hurt was a fact of life, and they had no real modeling to teach them otherwise. Instead, they all learned to be codependent.

At the root of codependency is emotional dis-regulation, the disconnection between what one feels and what one expresses. When caregivers are not able to fulfill their own needs, when they are living outside of their own arousal zones, they cannot help but pass on their own emotional baggage. They carry these old stories and behaviors and fixed action patterns into the family system because they themselves have not had the self care to process their own feelings and issues. Because they lack their own emotional harmony, they too are confined by a role they have agreed to play, often becoming agitated or dissociated with the circumstances in which they have found themselves. And these neurologically impressionable children are watching this demonstration, picking up cues, behavioral patterns, and habits along the way.

Instead, we learn to compensate and control to make up for the values we failed to learn as children. The emotionally dis-regulated family emphasizes the outsides versus the insides, because it has not fostered the value of one's self-worth. When Cathy began journaling about her family history, her mother found some of the writings wherein Cathy described her relationship with her mother as "distant but cordial."

Her mother was aghast, and immediately called one of Cathy's sisters to complain that Cathy's therapeutic work was going to "make [Cathy's mother] look like a bad person." For the codependent there is nothing more important than how they "look." This dis-regulated family system believes that only money or power or prestige in the community, no matter how small the community, is what is of value. They believe that in order to have a worthwhile identity, you must gain approval from the outside world, judged upon social cues, people's impressions, and cultural norms. This codependency creates what Sharon Wegscheider-Cruse, therapist and author of *Another Chance*, calls a "family trap," wherein family members are designated certain roles, playing them through their childhood and into their adult lives. As Sharon explains, there are six major roles in the emotionally dis-regulated family system:

1. The Addict – this person either suffers from a chemical or process addiction. It can be an addiction to alcohol or drugs, or an addiction to work, love, debting, or any number of behavioral processes that take on an addictive power over the individual. The addict suffers inwardly from fear, shame, and guilt, but externally exhibits charm, perfectionism, and excuses. For Cathy, the addict was her father and husbands whose own addictions took center stage over the health and well-being of those around them.

2. The Enabler – The enabler is there to support and protect the addict, often exchanging their own self-worth and physical health to create a false sense of security in the household. Though they inwardly have anger, they often act as the over-responsible protector, the rescuer, the super-worker, even though they might simultaneously appear ill and fragile, demanding attention where and how they can.

3. The Hero – Often the eldest child, the hero's job is to people please, aiming to take the focus off of the family secrets through their own success and drive. For Cathy,

her eldest sister Jacki played this role. After high school, Jacki received a scholarship to an Ivy League school, ultimately earning a Ph.D. Though she was often the most tormented by their father, she strived to be the best student, and the best behaved because lurking underneath all those achievements, was a girl who believed she was ultimately guilty and inadequate.

4. The Scapegoat – Often the second child in the family, the scapegoat is also always seeking attention away from the addict but does so through rebellious behavior, self-destructing to avoid the hurt they carry inside.

5. The Lost Child – This was Cathy in her family system. Withdrawn, shy, a low achiever in school despite her high test scores, she suffered a deep loneliness and a sense of withdrawal from an early age. Seeking escape in books and fantasy, she found herself socially isolated and confused, an easy mark for a love and sex-addicted man looking for a partner.

6. The Mascot – Often the youngest child, this role is characterized by its outward attention seeking, humor, and hyper activity. The mascot gets away with things the other children can't but still lives in the same inward fear, often suffering from immaturity and emotional illnesses well into adulthood.

And then we grow up, and we bring those same patterns into our adult relationships. For Cathy, she experienced that sense of longing for what it might be like to be held and embraced by the family system around her, and when she met Bill, she thought she had found it. He was a gentle and quiet man, and doted on her lovingly. Even in their final days, Bill would romance her, bringing her flowers and slow dancing with her in the living room after the children had fallen asleep. He was a very adept seducer and perpetrator – offering her the love and comfort for which she had ached her entire childhood and then making her pay for it by sexually abusive behavior and infidelity. Just as in Stockholm syndrome, where the victims express empathy for their captors, those captors use the intrinsic qualities of a person against them. I am always reminded of the movie, "The Green Mile," in which two sisters are abducted and refuse to leave each other, which ultimately leads to their demise. The perpetrator tells the sisters that he will kill the other one if she tells of his abuse. Ultimately, he murders them both. As the character John Coffey explains later, "He killed them with their love."

For many love addicts, this is exactly what happens. They get destroyed by their own love, by their own sweet vulnerabilities. But for many years, Cathy lived in the lie that something was better than nothing, and like most codependents, as long as everything looked okay on the outside, as long as the women at church envied their house, as long as their children did well in school and won at sports, as long as they presented the front of a happy and healthy family, no one had to know what happened at night.

These ruptured or insecure attachments of childhood have led my clients to seek codependent relationships in adulthood, often resulting in love and sex addiction. For many who walk into EHC, they may not realize that's going to end up being the focus of their work. They think they're coming into fix "him" or to make "her" happy. What they don't know is that the biggest issue is right in front of them—the elephant in the room—their own wounded attachment styles.

From watching the relationships in front of us, we develop these sexual/relational templates. For me, my mother was single for most of my childhood. I didn't see healthy sexual relationships—I didn't see *any* relationships—and I certainly didn't see any healthy modeling of gay men. Instead, I grew up emotionally anorexic and sexually confused. When romantic love is involved, it often includes expressions of one's sexuality, thus why love and sex addiction intertwine. For some clients, they are the partners of sex addicts, enabling the sexual behavior, though not instigating it. For others, however, their search for or avoidance of love leads to their own unhealthy sexual choices and addictive manifestations.

According to the *Sex and Love Addicts Anonymous*, there are twelve characteristics of sex and love addiction:

1. Having few healthy boundaries, we become sexually involved with and/or emotionally attached to people without knowing them. For Cathy, this took place in her six-week courtship by Bill. With little knowledge of whom this man really was, she entered into a sacred pact to be with him for the rest of her life.

2. Fearing abandonment and loneliness, we stay in and return to painful, destructive relationships, concealing our dependency needs from ourselves and others, growing more isolated and alienated from friends and loved ones, ourselves and God. Cathy's relationships continued to remove her from any outside healthy community, thus isolating her and her relationship.

3. Fearing emotional and/or sexual deprivation, we compulsively pursue and involve ourselves in one relationship after another, sometimes having more than one sexual or emotional liaison at a time. Within months of her divorce being finalized, Cathy met Chris. A Baptist divorcee himself, she felt that he would understand and be the man she had been waiting for.

4. We confuse love with neediness, physical and sexual attraction, pity and/or the need to rescue or be rescued. Bill rescued Cathy from the memories and pains of her father, and then Chris rescued her from the memories and pains of Bill, both of whom used sex as their means to communicate emotionally.

5. We feel empty and incomplete when we are alone. Even though we fear intimacy and commitment, we continually search for relationships and sexual contacts. Cathy could not bear the thought of being alone; her identity had always been entangled with another's.

6. We sexualize stress, guilt, loneliness, anger, shame, fear and envy. We use sex or emotional dependence as substitutes for nurturing, care, and support. Cathy often confused sex with love, initiating intimacy when she didn't feel like she was getting the love or attention she wanted.

7. We use sex and emotional involvement to manipulate and control others. For Cathy, she would often say no to one sexual act with Bill, only to acquiesce in order to get his attention back.

8. We become immobilized or seriously distracted by romantic or sexual obsessions or fantasies. From an early age, fantasy had been Cathy's escape, and into her adult life, it was no different. She frequently dreamed about the relationship she could have with her husbands, not the one she did.

9. We avoid responsibility for ourselves by attaching ourselves to people who are emotionally unavailable. Though both Chris and Bill were outwardly romantic, inwardly they were both emotionally dis-regulated men who could not be relied upon for a true, healthy attachment.

10. We stay enslaved to emotional dependency, romantic intrigue, or compulsive sexual activities. For Cathy, she was sexually enslaved by Bill for twenty years, and then Chris romantically for five. She had never been free to have her own emotional, romantic, or sexual identity.

11. To avoid feeling vulnerable, we may retreat from all intimate involvement, mistaking sexual and emotional anorexia for recovery. Cathy didn't know how to be

emotionally involved with a man in a healthy, balanced manner—resorting to extreme intimacy or none at all.

12. We assign magical qualities to others. We idealize and pursue them, then blame them for not fulfilling our fantasies and expectations. Cathy had grown up with a father who pretended to be God—the ultimate judge and juror in their household. It wasn't hard for her to assign the same roles to her husbands, believing them to the Princes of her fantasies, and not real men with real fears and abusive behaviors.

Take a moment and see where those characteristics show up in your life today, and where they show up in your family of origin. Because sadly, for many of us, we are born into sick families where we learn this codependency. We learn to take care of others instead of ourselves, and we learn to adapt our Authentic Selves to the demands of the unhealthy relational templates around us. The whole system embodies this way of doing relationships because the whole becomes more than the sum of its parts. The system in turn coalesces and adjusts around the disorder in the home. And so the people in that system are forced to create an Adaptable Self because, if their truths are in conflict with the rules and expectations of the family system, they will no longer be able to function within it. In an emotionally dis-regulated family, when the child senses it isn't safe to express their Authentic Selves, they mold and adapt themselves to the system around them, shielding their authentic selves from the outside world.

Then we wake up thirty years later, trapped in a web of love and sex addiction, wondering how we got ourselves there in the first place.

"He was *just* violent"

Many years back, Cathy remembers a conversation she had with her mother about her father:

> *My mother and I worked together later in life, and I remember we were doing the flowers for my daughter's wedding. We were watching a daytime talk show and it was about violence and incest and she said, "I wonder if your father ever molested any of you." And I said, "No, he was just violent." She stopped and stared at me, with a confused look on her face, replying, "No he wasn't. He was just strict."*

When Cathy was seven years old, she broke an old, unused vase while playing in the family basement. Her father heard the commotion, and when he saw what she had done, he lifted her by her shirt and began to slam her into the basement wall. She remembered her head hitting the brick wall a number of times before her memory went black, either slipping into unconsciousness or dissociation. Most likely, both.

We learn to bond to other humans through the attachments we have with our primary care givers: our parents. It forms the foundation for all the relationships to come. These attachments can be secure—based in trust and safety—or they can look like the attachments of Cathy's childhood, insecure and disorganized, creating only heightened arousal or fearful collapse.

In a series of experiments conducted by psychologist Harry Harlow between 1957 and 1963 at the University of Wisconsin-Madison, Harlow removed baby rhesus monkeys from their mothers and arranged for them to be "raised" by two kinds of surrogate monkey mother machines, both equipped to dispense milk. One device was made out of bare mesh wire. The other was fashioned from wire and covered with soft terrycloth. It was found that the young monkeys clung to the terrycloth mother whether or not it provided them with food, finding that the attachment was more important than the food.

Our need for attachment is one of the keys to our survival. We would die without the love and care that parents are intended to provide, which is why we are willing to accept any kind of behavior as care. Even years later, Cathy would describe her father as being "just" violent, despite years of physical abuse.

In a secure attachment, we are given what we need and want to survive. Coming from that place of consistency and safety, we are empowered to explore the world and to find our own identity. It is the difference between an abused dog and a well-loved one. A well-loved, well-trained dog will always approach a human with confidence and kindness. An abused dog will approach with fear and, possibly, aggression. Unfortunately, many of us behave like the latter.

With an insecure attachment, we are taught the dance of love addiction. We are either enmeshed in the relationship or trying to avoid it. As a parenting style, these attachment dynamics influence the relational templates for the children that can set a trajectory for life. For the parent who is anxious or avoidant, the child will experience those conditions as love. In turn, these children grow up to mimic the pattern in other relationships, recreating either avoidant or enmeshment dynamics in their adult relationships. In disorganized attachments, primary caregivers exhibit both styles of insecure attachment—sometimes they're avoidant, sometimes they're enmeshed—resulting in more intense, chaotic, and intense dynamics in the love addiction pattern.

The love avoidant will try to keep people at arm's length while privately longing to be pursued in a relationship. But when they find themselves in a relationship and the commitment deepens, they'll retreat from intimacy in an attempt to soothe their own activation. Avoidants orchestrate the addicts' engulfment. And this is what many of us call love.

In my own upbringing, I lived under the insecure attachment I had formed with my mother, where I would try to take care of her in order to receive love and comfort, and when I was unable to get the attention I was seeking, I would become angry. I still remember being five years old and knowing that my mother was so tired whenever she came home from work, I decided I would do the dishes for her. I was standing on a chair and I was washing the dishes by hand and I was getting so excited because when mom came home she was going to be so happy because I did the dishes. I made it my job to make my mother happy, and if she wasn't happy, that too was my doing. When I wouldn't receive the attention I craved, I would react by throwing tantrums, telling her how I hated her. I felt absolutely enmeshed, unable to tell where the boundaries were between us. Parents don't do this to be harmful. Sadly, many of us come from generations of trauma and codependence.

"They're doing the best they can with what they got"

Recently, I had a client tell me a story about his grandfather who was a Holocaust survivor—a hardened man for whom much of his life had been lost before he turned twenty years old. But the old man could still remember back to a gentler time, before the war, when he remembered the warmth of his own grandfather's hand in the shtetl. There the older generations expressed physical affection openly, amongst husband and wife, between parent and child. But after the war, all that changed. The tenderness, which had once defined them, had been systemically ripped apart and away from their culture.

As Michelle explains, if parents don't do the work that needs to be healed neurologically and emotionally, they can't help but pass it along to the next generation. As Michelle describes, in her own family history, her grandparents who came out of the

Holocaust and the Depression passed along the fear and trauma of their circumstances: "Though they came out of it, they didn't do any of the emotional recovery work, so many of my family members raised their children disengaged and not attached to them."

If you have a generation of people who have experienced traumas, and therefore are doing relationships from ruptured places, they're going to attach and parent from an impaired attachment style. That pattern is then handed down from one generation to the next, creating and perpetuating what clinically is known as generational trauma. As with most people, they're "doing the best they can with what they got" until they are willing to do something different.

And though not everyone's family holds such systemic trauma, abusive and insecure attachments are often passed down between generations.

"It was like I lived my whole life slamming in and out of my body"

When one is raised in a secure attachment, he or she learns how to regulate their emotional world. They are given life tools that help them withstand difficulties and celebrate joys. They are taught that self-worth is born within, fostered in an environment where the adults live lives of high self-worth as well. They are equipped with the resiliency to repair from life's tribulations.

But if the child is raised within insecure or disorganized attachments, they are not taught how to regulate their emotions. These attachment disorders can begin prenatally, as we are now able to glimpse with 3 dimensional ultrasound. There are a lot of studies going on today on the role of a mother's emotions on her unborn fetus. If you have a mother who is dis-regulated emotionally and is pregnant, how does the stress of her daily life affect the child growing inside her? How is she going to be able to form a secure and confident attachment to the baby when she herself lives in insecurity and fear? We are still learning some of the ramifications of this common problem. If you have a parent who did not receive their own attunement by a caregiver, how can they be expected to pass on that which they didn't get themselves? The awesome emotional responsibility of parenting can be overwhelming for anyone, but for someone who lives in emotional dis-regulation, it would be nearly impossible not to be overwhelmed by the task.

If the caregiver is dis-regulated, their own nervous system is challenged to meet the needs of the child. Without the ability to maintain their Optimal Arousal Zone, the parent is unable to create an environment where healthy self-regulation is modeled. In turn, the infant fails to develop resiliency capabilities to deal with life's stressors.

So that child grows up, similarly overwhelmed by the successes and trials of life. Coming from these insecure attachments, the person learns to live in either a state of *hyper* arousal, where anxiety and fear are the norm, or *hypo* arousal, where detachment and numbness are common. For some, they live vacillating between these two states, unable to find balance. Whether one is living in activation, collapse, or both, they will need to attach to something to create the illusion of emotional control. They will find food, nicotine, alcohol, drugs, sex, and other emotional medicators in an attempt to soothe the feelings held as a result of these insecure primary attachments.

As Cathy explained to me, "I could be dissociating and panicking at the same time. I lived in a disassociate state, to the point where the numbness was normal, and yet I could be sobbing at the same time. It was as though I was constantly slamming in and out of my body."

It's no wonder we get sick. I was a mess when I finally got sober. I didn't know whether to laugh, cry, or have a raging fit. I had stopped having feelings for so long that when those feelings returned, they took me over in uncontrollable waves. Finally, my therapist asked me, "What are you so angry about?" *Angry*, I thought, *I don't even know what that means.* Anger was intolerable and unacceptable in my family, but the truth was those adaptable qualities that I considered to be part of my "edginess" or my intensity were really just consequences of the chasm between myself and my emotional truth. Since I had made that commitment in sobriety to be honest no matter what, I had to start looking at where that anger was coming from. Though I didn't know how to identify it, I certainly was angry.

I began to explore how unhealthy attachments to certain processes and behaviors were keeping me from loving myself. I was willing to recognize the insecure attachments and codependent modeling that had been the foundation of my emotional life. I started asking questions, hard questions, and I started drawing boundaries for myself. Boundaries that had never been drawn for me. I understood that this work was about a lot more than getting sober; it was about finally telling the truth, telling *my* truth, so that one day, if I decided to have children, I would be able to pass down a new set of values—not the worn-out hand me downs that had been traded for generations, but new ones, based in the concepts of healthy families, in healthy partnership, free of the codependency and addiction that had gripped my family system for decades.

Looking at your own family history, where have you seen some of the following:

- Does your family have an active higher power?
- Does your family live in fear?
- Do they teach fear of others regarding race, religion, color, nationality, etc.?
- Do they believe that you "must do it for yourself?"

- Do they believe that to be happy, healthy, and successful, you must make, marry, or have money?
- Do they believe the family should stick together and depend on each other to the exclusion of the outside world, unless the family finds an outside that is identical to themselves?
- Does your family believe that in order to have a worthwhile identity, you must gain approval from the outside world, especially the approval of the family itself?
- Do they teach that the authority figures in your family are always right?
- Do they teach that marriage completes the identity of individual?
- Does your family feel the "flow of achievement" when a member of the family does well, and do they feel let down when a member does "badly?"
- Do they teach each member to adapt to the sickness of the group?
- Do they feel threatened when a one of the family members seeks outside help?
- Does your family feel totally abandoned at the death or departure of a loved member of the group?
- Does your family try to hold themselves together through guilt and pity, which is called "love?"
- Do they create unreal expectations of one another?
- Does your family believe that everyone within the group should like the same things and the same people?
- Is your family conditioned by the beliefs and experiences of the past, unable to live in a serene and peaceful present?
- Do they only perceive a fearful future?
- Do they thrive on excitement and teach through intensity?
- Does your family have fights, arguments, violence, hate, criticism, grief, lust, resentments, jealousies, fantasies, anger, depression, euphoria—yet teach unconditional love?

If you have answered yes to three or more of these questions, it might be time for you start looking at the relationships in your own life, the attachments you share with your family of origin, and those you've made by choice. It might be time stop the emotionally dis-regulated family tradition and start creating relationships with people who nurture and support your Authentic Self. Instead of mirroring those behaviors of the past, we have the opportunity to make conscious, realized choices for our present and to set real, vivid goals as we begin to move towards emotional harmony.

BRAIN BASICS WITH MICHELLE:
THE TRIUNE BRAIN

In Dan Siegel's book *Mindsight*, he describes what many now refer to as the Triune Brain, the evolutionary model of the vertebrate forebrain. The Triune Brain was first proposed by neuroscientist Paul D. MacLean in the 1960s as a way to describe the functioning components of the forebrain. Though its evolutionary process has been disputed in recent years, it still remains one of our best models of understanding how the different parts of the brain interact.

Siegel offers a simple description to understand MacLean's model:

> If you put your thumb in the middle of your palm and then curl your fingers over the top, you'll have a pretty handy model of the brain. The forehead of the person is in front of the knuckles, the back of the head is toward the back of the hand, down your wrist. Your wrist represents the spinal cord, rising from your backbone, upon which the brain sits. If you lift up your fingers and raise your thumb, you'll see the inner brainstem represented in your palm. Place your thumb back down and you'll see the approximate location of the limbic area (ideally we'd have two thumbs,

left and right, to make this a symmetric model). Now curl your fingers back over the top, and your cortex is in place.

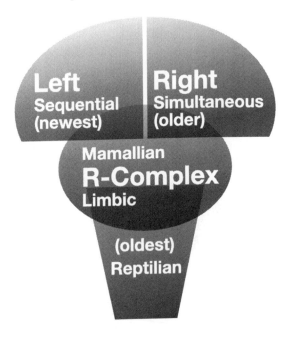

The Triune Brain is made up of three regions, debated to have been developed over the course of evolution: the brainstem, the limbic area—which includes the left and right hemispheres—and the cortex. The brain stem comes from the oldest part of the brain and oversees all basic primary functions, including muscle, balance, and autonomic functions, such as breathing and heart rate. Often called the reptilian brain, the brain stem is the first region to develop in-utero. The brain stem functions without intention or thought, requiring no outside control over things like breathing or heartbeat. Then you go into the limbic system, which is often called the Paleomammalian brain. According to our hand model, the thumb is the limbic system. This is the emotional center of the brain. Most emotion is processed up from the body through the brainstem, the right hemisphere, and into the limbic system. When we are activated during fight, flight or freeze, it is this system that gets triggered. It helps determine valence – your ability to judge an event as positive or negative – and salience – which helps you to determine what should get your attention. The purpose of this is to achieve safety. Eventually, the limbic system connects into the neocortex, however this is the last portion to come on line in a moment of fear. It can even be after the event in the form of trying to "make sense" of why something happened. This is a common experience for trauma survivors.

Then you have your neocortex, which includes your prefrontal cortex, the front of the knuckles in our hand model. The prefrontal cortex isn't utilized until a child is between eighteen months and two years old. It houses higher executive thinking, and is also divided into left and right hemispheres. The right brain is more spatial, abstract, musical and artistic, while the left-brain is more linear, rational, and verbal.

In a developed brain all these parts are working in harmony. This harmony allows for an expanded consciousness, a heightened intellectual ability, and an embodied and empathic lived experience. Ideally we want these different parts working in coherence and cooperation, and not in cohesion, separate and at odds with one another. For trauma survivors some of these functions can become very rigid as a way to try and " make sense" of a tragedy that happened. The extreme versions of this can look like OCD symptoms—counting, not stepping on cracks, never flying on an airplane—all in an attempt to control the fear state and preventing the harmonious flow of feelings and experiences tolerated in the body and brain. This dis-regulation is like a wall between the parts of the system instead of a border. Information and experience become compartmentalized. In order for healing to occur, these different parts need to begin integrating. We need to be able to create a relationship between the different parts of the brain so that we will be better able to experience the events

CHAPTER TWO

Big T and Little T

According to psychologist and noted trauma expert Peter Levine, "Trauma is the most avoided, ignored, denied, misunderstood, and untreated cause of human suffering." And perhaps the most difficult aspect of this human suffering is that we all experience it differently. For one person, it might be the trauma from a childhood accident that has led them to live in a dis-regulated emotional state. Someone else might have experienced a similar tragedy, and he or she was able to recover and repair from it. I know that for Michelle and I, we both were affected by trauma as children, but the bigger issue was not the actual event or external stimuli, it was how we learned to manage our reactions that ultimately determined the level of suffering we experienced and our ability to heal.

At Experiential Healing Center (EHC), our goal is to help people experience such repair, and we have found that one of the most powerful ways to renegotiate that trauma is through the reconstruction process. Reconstructions are a committed recovery effort involving a comprehensive excavation and exploration of a person's timeline and autobiography. Unfortunately, for many of us, our biography becomes our biology. That life story changes how we physiologically experience and react to the world around us. Through the reconstruction process, we reconstruct the biography so that we may begin to re-negotiate the ruptures experienced in trauma. As part of this process, we take time to collect and integrate the parts of a client's story while using various resources available including but not limited to autobiographies, genograms, music playlists, and timelines of their lives. Many clients do this comprehensive work just as part of their therapy, while others might decide to incorporate and celebrate it through the process of a Reconstruction Day. That being said, everyone who embarks on a reconstruction process is committing to a powerful and comprehensive therapeutic experience.

When Cathy was preparing for her "recon," as we call it, I asked that she first write her entire life autobiography, charting as many memories as she could throughout her childhood into adolescence. In hers she wrote of her first memory of life:

> *I am in a big bed with a heavy red comforter on top. I can hear Grandma cooking in the kitchen. I hear Grandpa tell the other girls to come along; it's time to go. I jump up and pull my clothes on and grab my shoes. They are already out the door and walking across the field. I sit down on the porch to put on my shoes. I get one on but they are too far away. I am afraid I will not be able to catch up. I pick up my shoe and run across the grass, hollering for them to wait. They look back, but keep walking. My foot is on fire. I scream and jump around on the other foot, then fall to the grass and hold my burning foot, wailing uncontrollably. Grandpa runs back to me and takes my foot in his hand. He shows me a tiny black thorn in my foot and tells me I have been stung by a bee. He picks me up and carries me gently back to the house. Grandma gives me an ice cube to hold on the white spot in the middle of the big red swelling on the bottom of my foot. She cuts an onion in half and tells me to keep rubbing it over the same spot. Grandpa*

and the girls wait for me before we leave again to go pick blueberries.

This memory was one amongst many others gathered by Cathy over a lifetime—an idyllic response to a childhood bee sting. If only all of Cathy's life experiences had been negotiated so well. This memory was one of her more resourceful, offering her an experience where repair and recovery were possible; where fear was responded to with concern and relief replaced pain.

Sadly, many more memories prevailed, offering very different messages. Just as in mine. Just as in yours. There are two types of major trauma, which both children and adults can experience. The first is developmental or attachment trauma, which occurs in a chronic, ongoing way, often over the course of one's childhood or over a period of time. This trauma may involve abandonment, physical or sexual abuse, or neglect. For some, the abuse never took on a physical form but was just as detrimental: emotional abuse, witnessing violence or death, or being asked to participate in coercion or betrayal against one or both parents. Unfortunately, many of us were raised by parents who were emotionally wounded themselves, unaware of how their behaviors would affect their ability to attach and communicate with their impressionable and neurologically-vulnerable offspring.

The second form of trauma is shock trauma, Big-T trauma, which often takes place within the space of one event or time period, startling and suddenly breaching the boundaries of self. These events violate one's sense of security or identity, and can show up in many different landscapes, such as the Holocaust, 9/11, random violence, illness, car accidents, and any number of overt tragedies. But why do some walk away from a car accident able to live normal and healthy lives while others struggle to emotionally repair from the experience? These are the questions that can be answered through SomEx^SM. By identifying those fixed action patterns that create barriers to repair, we can create new ways to manage the effects of trauma.

"I didn't get any cake"

Just as physical abuse, abandonment, rape, disaster, and any number of other Big T traumas can wage their wars on childhood and later life, so can the more subtle events of dis-regulated emotion—what we call the "little t" traumas. According to Robert Alan Schwarz in *Tools for Transforming Trauma*, "A little t trauma is an event that is beyond a person's ability to master at the time of the event. It can be something as simple as a child getting lost for a few minutes, or a child being overwhelmed with fear after a nightmare and no one comforting the child. These little t traumas often are left unprocessed in the unconscious. They create areas of vulnerability that make it more difficult to handle when Big T trauma occurs."

Relational trauma is often the effect of chronic, ongoing, cumulative stress as the result of our attachments to parents and caregivers. For so many of us, our lives are interspersed with this tension. I remember my sister once describing how my mother would feed me when I was a baby. She would lean back in the chair exhausted and overwhelmed, her hand extended with a bottle, while I sat propped in front of her. I believe I always "saw" the sadness in her eyes, failing to receive the appropriate soothing and bonding that would have happened were it not for the trauma in our family. Over the course of my childhood, I experienced an ongoing insecure attachment to my mother due to the coupling of her emotional pain with my need for bonding and attachment. This wasn't out of any conscious effort on her part to wound or abuse. I know in my mother's heart she wanted to love us the best she could, but that potential was stunted by her own woundedness and lack of attunement, preventing her from having emotional harmony in her own life.

Cathy's life provided similar obstacles. She remembers another small "t" in her world, another moment at her grandparents' ranch, but one that better reflected her environment at home:

> *We are at the ranch. It is a big white house in the middle of a large field. Grandma and lots of other people are there. Mary and Jacki are cutting a big cake and I offer to help serve it. They give me two plates at a time and I carry them to people in the house. I go back over and over again to get cake and take it to other people. When I return to the kitchen, Mary and Jacki are eating cake, but there is none left. I say, "I didn't get any cake." Mary puts her face very close to mine. She smirks and talks in a whiney voice saying, "Oh you poor pitiful little thing. You didn't get any cake. Boo hoo." I am scared and I turn and run out of the kitchen, Mary and Jacki's laughter echoing behind me.*

Now, if you had brothers and sisters, you've probably had your own fair share of sibling cruelty, but Cathy had spent her whole life crying, "I didn't get any cake." Years later, when we were in group therapy, there was a new client there, Melissa, who told Cathy that she behaved like a "victim." Cathy was beside herself and called another member of the group, and asked if she agreed. The other woman was hesitant, not wanting to hurt her friend and fellow group members' feelings, but finally confessed, "I'm sorry, honey, but yes, I think you've gotten quite good at playing that role." A lifetime of abuse will help you do that. Cathy was enraged, and called me, wanting to hear what I thought. I told her we should wait until the next group session and discuss it there.

It was agreed that we would begin with a family sculpt, wherein the different members of the group would role-play some of the characters in Cathy's life. I asked Cathy to choose one of the other members of the group to play herself.

The first question out of her mouth was, "Me as a child or me as a victim?"

I smiled. "Good question."

She asked Melissa to play "Victim Cathy."

"And where does Victim Cathy live?" I asked.

Cathy looked at me blankly and smiled. "Nepal. Antarctica. Somewhere far away."

Later she told me that she had grown up hating that victim part of herself and no wonder. She heard those childhood voices in her head singing, "You poor little pitiful thing. You didn't get any cake. Boo hoo."

As Cathy explained later, "I realized that until I could embrace that little girl, that same little girl who grew up into the adult-sized victim, she was going to keep making noise."

These little traumas play a role, often more significant than we give them credit for. They enter the fray of truths we have been told about ourselves, cementing the much bigger traumas that linger around them. We use these traumas as evidence of our own guilt. Blaming ourselves for the disordered attachments in our lives, we riddle our lives with the lie that suffering is the only way, and in turn, we create a belief system in which trauma becomes the normal state of being rather than an isolated event. Not only are we unable to create healthy attachments with others, we are unable to regulate our emotional relationship with ourselves, instead remaining attached to the dis-regulated belief system and/or environment in which the trauma thrives.

A regulated adult caregiver is an essential template for the infant/child's organization of their nervous system, helping that child to regulate and repair from the inevitable traumas of life. But when the patterns of development are interrupted in a child because of a lack of nurturing experiences, the nervous system of that child becomes overwhelmed and confused by the caregiver's lack of attunement. Writer Stephen Porges describes this scenario in his work, *The Polyvagal Theory*: "Essential development of brain fibers is not formed. Coherence and harmony are impaired. This influences all later cognitive emotional and relational abilities and creates less resilience to…trauma."

In a healthy brain, all parts of the brain structure function together, creating a coherent system of interpreting, processing and communicating emotional responses to external stimuli. But when trauma is introduced into the life a developing brain, these various brain functions, including the development of the nervous system, become disorganized and are unable to integrate information coherently. If there is healthy attunement, the child's autonomic nervous system will be able to respond and repair; without such attunement, the child will not be able to find safety, and he or she will move outside of their Optimal Arousal Zone.

In 2007, Dr. Ed Tronick of the University of Massachusetts at Boston demonstrated this through his "Still Face" Experiment, in which a mother denied her baby attention for a short period of time. Dr. Tronick's experiment aimed to show how lack of attention could shift an infant from a state of healthy socialization and attachment into one of confusion and threat. In the experiment, a mother comes into a room with her eighteen-month old. She communicates with the young child, making the usual facial cues one projects when greeting a baby. She is smiling, laughing and twisting her face into tender expressions of safety and love. Then the mother turns her back to the child. When she turns around, she makes no facial expressions whatsoever. In fact, she is still-faced—staring blankly at the baby and not responding verbally and not matching with her facial cues. At first the baby struggles with this concept, crooking its neck, it appears to be looking for her real mother. As the experiment continues, the baby gets more and more aroused—crying, squirming and ultimately screaming in response to her mother's changed disposition.

When a child is activated outside of their own healthy arousal zone, hopefully the caregiver is able offer them a place for repair and regulation. This is not about living in perfect balance at all times, but rather about being able to process our environments from an emotionally regulated space. As Michelle explains, a child who lives outside this zone is engaged in an ongoing activated state. Unsure of how to self-soothe, he or she will seek ways to escape or relieve the agitation that such a state creates, self-medicating through any number of processes. Before they start using alcohol or drugs, many addicts admit to being "addicted" to fantasy. This could come through seemingly innocent activities like reading books or engaging in daydreaming to more complex behaviors like masturbation and/or an excessive interest in romance or sexuality. Today, however, we see a lot of this self-soothing coming out in food and video games as children use the chemicals and processes available to them for escape. Every decade, the numbers seem to get worse. Children are growing up in a dis-regulated state and they are seeking means by which to cope with these imbalances, abusing whatever is at hand as a means to self-regulate.

As parents and caregivers, we need to recognize that safety is the most important aspect of regulating our autonomic nervous systems. Children and infants need signs from their environment that they are safe in order to be able process that environment in a clear and harmonious way. They need to know that their parents are there to pull out the bee stinger and to soothe them when they fail to get that last piece of cake.

"Hit her. Really hit her. Hit her hard."

And then there is Big T trauma. Big T trauma is defined by Francine Shapiro and Margot Silk Forrest in *EMDR: The Breakthrough Therapy for Overcoming Anxiety, Stress, and Trauma* to include "events that a person perceives as threatening; combat, crimes such as rape, kidnapping, and assault; and natural disasters such as earthquakes, tornadoes, fires, and flood. These events are so stressful they can overwhelm our ordinary capacity to cope. They result in intense fear, extreme feelings of helplessness, and a crushing loss of control."

Big T trauma can include many forms of abuse—physical, sexual, emotional, psychological—and it can relate to one large event, as in a shock trauma or a series of high-arousal scenarios that take place over time. For Cathy, her father's abuse was an ongoing, recurring traumatic experience that caused her to live either way above or way below her Optimal Arousal Zone. She created a pattern of response to these traumas, which skewed the regulation of her nervous system. In a healthy nervous system, one is able to oscillate between the boundaries of their Optimal Arousal Zone wherein they can experience a full range of emotions from a regulated and grounded place. People who are raised in traumatic environments will constrict the perimeter of their Optimal Arousal Zone, producing an adaptability and inflexibility around their reactions to life.

In a far cry from the memories on her grandparent's ranch, Cathy describes another story of her childhood:

> *Mary and I are arguing over a toy. One of us hits the other one, and we start to fight. Dad comes in and stands us in the middle of the room. He tells Mary to hit me. We both start to cry. He hollers, "Hit her!" Mary hits me, lightly on the arm. He says, "Hit her. Really hit her. Hit her hard." She hits me hard. He tells me to get her back as I begin to cry. I don't want to punch my big sister. "Hit her," he demands again. "Hit her hard." I punch her arm and we both cry. He makes us stand there punching each other hard several times as we beg for him to let us stop. Finally, he asks, "Do you want*

> *to hit each other or do you want to play?" We tell him*
> *that we want to play. And then, as though nothing has*
> *happened, he says, "Then go play."*

Cathy was eight years old. Mary was nine. I can only imagine them now in their bedroom, being forced to punch each other as they screamed and cried, their father demanding violent retribution for a typical childhood dispute over a toy.

When an animal experiences trauma, they will yelp and seize, often urinating or defecating in response to the event, releasing the fear and tension held by the body. In a recent study in Alaska, a group of scientists were tracking a polar bear by helicopter, hoping to tranquilize the bear for further examination. As they flew alongside the bear, they filmed the animal's attempts to outrun the strange flying machine. The animal is filmed looking back, orienting himself to the helicopter and his environment until he realizes that he cannot escape. Immediately slowing down and freezing, the animal "surrenders," before being shot by a tranquilizer gun. Once the tranquilizer wears off, however, the animal releases the trauma through a series of seizures. After his body finishes emitting the trauma, he sinks into deep, guttural breathing and a calmed state.

If only we humans were allowed such a response. Cathy and her siblings were consistently chased down by their father's violence, but there was no space held for that primitive release. They knew that to react would only engender more violence. Instead, they were sent out to play, to pretend that nothing had happened to them. They were trained to treat their trauma as routine, never being given a safe space in which to release the fear and tension, and to regulate their autonomic systems. Instead that trauma remained trapped in their cellular memory, creating patterns of reaction and behavior, which got replicated well into adulthood.

In many ways, this goes back to the still face exercise in which the baby was unable to orient and attune itself to the environment because her caregiver was reflecting a disorganized attachment. Since babies have no way to communicate their discomfort, they will arch their backs and reach out, trying to communicate through their physical bodies. This is the concept of primitive defense—a human's ability to respond to an unsafe environment through pushing, reaching, and arching, much as an animal would do. Again, remember that the prefrontal cortex does not even come online until eighteen months, so at this point, we are only able to communicate from the reptilian state. When a young child is confronted with a life-threatening trauma or even an insecure attachment with a caregiver, they do not have a stable foundation from which to safely respond and repair.

These traumas can begin as early as in utero when the unborn child is feeding off the chemicals the mother is producing as she moves through pregnancy. A stressed and emotionally dis-regulated mother is passing that duress along to her child. Through her emotional chemistry and neurological reactions, she is inducing either a safe and flexible environment for the child to grow, or one in which fear is transmitted from mother to unborn babe. Then we are born, and through the proceeding years, we can face any number of traumatic incidents. But why do some survive and thrive, and others find themselves sitting on a couch much like the one I have in my office, asking, "What is wrong with me?"

Simply put, it is our ability to properly respond and repair that allows us to heal.

Over the course of their lives, many people are put in a position in which they are unable to respond to trauma. Withdrawing and collapsing, they act much like the polar bear caught on video, ultimately resigning themselves to whatever fate is being offered by their environment. You often see this in abusive relationships. The perpetrator will abuse the victim, and though the victim could physically fight back or leave, they ultimately relent. Conceding to the dissociation, they, like the polar bear, give up and give into the abuse. When this abuse happens in childhood, however, that person has even less of a choice. Learning to adapt to the abuse, they grow up without the ability to process intense emotions. Instead, they either submit, sinking into withdrawal, or they become so emotionally activated, they seek outside substances and processes to contain their emotional state.

When Cathy was growing up, she and her siblings would flinch any time their father would reach for the salt, fearing he was reaching for them instead. Later in her relationship with her first husband Bill, she at once craved and feared his affections. As she later described their relationship, "We had a cycle where, sexually, I would do whatever he wanted me to do for a long period, and then finally I wouldn't be able to take it anymore, and I would throw a fit, refusing to participate in his sexual behaviors. Some time would pass then where he would leave me alone, and then I would be the one to approach him sexually, offering the one thing I said I wasn't going to do."

She replaced one cycle of violence with another, creating the same bond she had experienced in childhood. Trauma patterns are created neurologically over time, woven together through repeated experience and abuse. If I grow up in a house where my caregiver is not attuned or attending to my needs, I am going to feel isolated and separate from those around me. Likewise, for Cathy, she grew up in a household where love was synonymous with boundary violations, and later sought that same trauma pattern in her interpersonal relationships. When someone says, "I married my father" or "I married my mother," many of them had little choice. They were neurologically wired to seek the same patterns of attachment they experienced in childhood. For some, this is a healthy attachment with a stable partner who mirrors the secure parenting they received as children, but for others, it is simply a re-enactment of the abuse and attachment disorders experienced in childhood.

"Dad starts laughing and I feel relieved"

One of the identifying features of a trauma bond is when captors create the right chemistry of loving care and attention mixed with randomly punctuated threats, violence, and degrading behavior. This relationship is identified by its own particular pattern between captor and captive. For most, it would be easier if the captor were vile all the time, then the victim would be able to identify the perpetrator as untrustworthy and break any emotional alliance created between them. But abuse is enacted on a variable reinforcement schedule in which the victim never knows when they are being tricked and when they might be treated. For most children in abusive households, the perpetrator is at times generous and loving, offering glimpses of the healthy parenting all children need, but the threat of abuse is always lurking under the kind words and gentle affection. In these relationships, often the anticipation of the abuse can seem worse than its actualization. As Cathy describes one confusing episode of her childhood:

> *I am sitting at the dinner table. I am wearing a Hawaiian print shirt-and-short set that mom has sewn for me. We have a Kool-Aid pitcher with the face on it. It has grape Kool-Aid in it. I ask for it to be passed to me. It is full and has ice in it. Mom asks if I need help. I say no, I can do it. I stand up to pour myself some Kool-Aid and I dump the whole pitcher out on the floor and myself. I burst into tears because I am afraid Dad is mad. Dad starts laughing and I feel relieved.*

Though trauma bonds may be formed instantaneously, they can last forever, creating a behavioral pattern in the abused person's life wherein emotional regulation is nearly impossible. As noted author and psychotherapist Felicity de Zulueta explains in *From Pain to Violence*, "In traumatic states of helplessness, both responses are hyper-activated...leading to an inward flight or dissociative response."

For Cathy, she became the silent child, the one who worked strenuously to not be the victim of her father's blows. Likewise, she grew up to become a willing and loyal captor in her sexually and emotionally abusive marriage, trained since childhood to detach from the abuse in order to accept it. As Patrick Carnes explains about his own relationship to trauma in his seminal work *The Betrayal Bond*, "Over time I learned that I bonded with people who were very hurtful to me and remained loyal to them despite betrayal and exploitation. This pattern of insane loyalty affected my professional and business relationships, my friendships, my finances and my intimate relationships... The problem is called trauma bonding. Betrayal intensifies pathologically the human trait of bonding deeply in the presence of danger or fear."

Cathy found that bond with Bill and, later, with Chris. Bill and she courted it and built it up as they did their first home, honing the details of their trauma bond. With each new sexual act, with each "no" from Cathy's mouth that later became a frustrated "yes," she deepened her loyalty to Bill's betrayal. By the time he finally got around to having affairs, she was primed for his infidelities. She had been trained for them since childhood. And in many ways, they only increased her loyalty. She told me later, "I was ready to leave him before he had the affair. I had this super huge loyalty to marriage, and I remember praying to God that He let me find a way out of the marriage. And then I found out he was having an affair, and I started fighting for him. Not long after, however, he would do something to the children, or me and I would say I was out, but before I knew it, he would return, begging to come home, and I would be right back into it. My sister finally said, 'Cathy, its like your addicted to him.'"

No shit. That addiction had been set up since childhood. Cathy could not have been attracted to a healthy person, because she had not been given a healthy sexual/relational template on how to attach.

"I'm Gone"

Trauma constricts our brain's ability to have coherence and fluidity between the left and right hemispheres, interrupting the natural processes by which we comprehend and interpret external and internal stimuli. Instead, we end up like one of those trees at Home Depot whose roots are so tightly wound you could knock it over with a light push. Trauma survivors have never been able to appropriately root their emotional processes. I know that for me, I could have been tipped over by the slightest prompt. When I was 7 or 8, I would throw anger fits, yelling and screaming until I would see illuminating specs in my eyes, escalating to a place where I could not be controlled. Maybe in another household this aggression would have been responded to with a healthier, more flexible communication, but in my house you could be happy or silent; there was no tolerance for other emotions. So I learned to express all emotions as anger, and ultimately, I learned to use alcohol to dissociate myself from any emotions at all.

It is the body's inclination to have a vibrant, diverse way of having emotions. Upon birth, the right hemisphere of our brain begins to develop in relationship to our caregiver. This process takes place over the first three years wherein the right hemisphere becomes the home of implicit memory and imagination, communicating with the limbic systems and the sensory motor aspects of the body. Whereas the left hemisphere is linear and logical, determined to make meaning, the right hemisphere doesn't have that same kind of organization. It is more mosaic, a divergent tapestry of conflicting emotional imprints and sensory suggestions.

The left hemisphere begins a little later, developing around eighteen months of age with the emergence of language. Unlike the right hemisphere, which is poly-semantic, able to house multiple meanings and understandings of the same stimulus, the left side is mono-semantic, searching for data to support logical, sequential meaning making. Though the left hemisphere is connected to the right through the corpus colosseum, in early developmental trauma, children disassociate from the right brain and create safety in left hemispheric functioning. Because the left hemisphere needs to draw on the right hemisphere in order to make sense of body and emotion—of those neurological imprints from the outside world—it becomes dissociated when the relationship between the two hemispheres is compromised. This is what we call cohesion, which often results in the experience of operating outside of the Optimal Arousal Zone.

The natural order of feeling progression is to feel something internally, express it externally, receive validation for the feeling, seek some kind of resolution, and then move towards acceptance of the outcome. If only we behaved and processed emotion in such a clean and linear fashion, and if we were regulated emotionally, more often than not, we would. Unfortunately when the left and right hemispheres are not integrated, we are unable to process our environment in a harmonious way. Though we want to be able to experience ourselves and make meaning of our emotions, the experience is so overwhelming to the system that we are neither able to comprehend nor communicate the emotional process. That's where dissociation comes in the whole body slows, blood pressure drops, and our ability to experience and process our sensory experience becomes muddled. Unable to make meaning out of the stimuli, we instead adapt to the environment, changing our moral standards or compromising our belief systems in order to accept the unacceptable. When people can't feel and are unable to express those feelings, they find medicators—substances and processes to change or alter their moods—that allow them to bridge that space between their feelings and their logical understanding of them. Cultures that support and encourage expression of emotion are better able to process these feelings, but for many of us, we grew up in families whose version of grief was to either cry in private or take a Valium.

Cathy lived most of her life in this dissociative gap. In one of her family sculpts, she was doing work around her first husband. One of her group members played the role of Bill, helping her to recreate one of their conversations around his infidelity. Suddenly Cathy began to cry, begging "Bill" to hold her. I suggested that the group member playing Bill refuse, wrapping his arms around himself instead. Cathy slumped down on the ground and said, "I'm gone."

"No," I explained. "You're here, Cathy. Can you notice your feet right now? Can you move them against the floor? Do you notice how that is? How do you experience me next to you? You're here. You're crying. You are having feelings."

But Cathy just shook her head, "No, I'm gone. I might be crying, but I am gone."

Cathy explained later that she could move into that dissociative state and the only thing that could bring her out of it was to be touched.

The fourth out of seven children, Cathy found herself sandwiched between her younger brother, who was born ten months after her, and her older sister, who was born a year before. As she told me later, "I wasn't held as a child, and by doing that work around Bill, I realized those feelings came from my infancy where I could feel in my soul that lack of connection, that place in me that just wanted to be soothed. I had just wanted Bill to fix that, to make it better, and when he couldn't, when my family couldn't, I felt like I was fading away."

The dissociation that takes place between our brain's two hemispheres is not just a breach in how we process emotion, but in how we connect to others, forming the basis of our attachment disorders.

"I became my depressed mother"

Well holy shit, so did I. In fact, we are all at risk of becoming our depressed mothers. Or fathers. Or grandparents, aunts, uncles, or siblings. When there are no boundaries to separate us from our caregivers, we end up emulating what we see. Unable to differentiate where they stop and where we begin, we create insecure and disorganized attachments with those who were entrusted to protect us. Though parents don't often recognize or understand the messaging they are offering, they are simultaneously developing the same insecure and disorganized attachments with their children. Though the words emotional incest have the ability to scare even the most therapeutized client, the truth is most of us grew up in homes where the relationships with our caregivers was not based on a healthy parent-child relational model, but rather on one where boundaries were blurred and the children were forced to act as caregivers.

According to Kenneth Adams in *Silently Seduced*, the characteristics of this emotional incest can include any of the following:

- The individual has a love/hate relationship between themselves and the opposite sex parent, and an emotional distance with their same-sex parent.
- The individual experiences guilt and confusion over their own needs, often confusing them with the needs of their family members. They feel inadequate and base their

esteem on what they are able to do, rather than who they are.

- The individual will have been in multiple relationships, without finding one that sustains them. They often have difficulty committing or make hasty commitments in relationships, recognizing the mistake after they have already made the commitment.

- The individual often has regret over past relationships, wondering what could have happened had they done things differently.

- The individual will have compulsions and addictions, particularly in regards to sex, where they will either be sexually compulsive or entirely shut down. They might also find themselves with other chemical and process addictions.

When a caregiver lives in their own unresolved woundedness, those emotionally dis-regulated experiences will be carried and processed by the children. Whether spoken or not, the parent's own traumas will be passed down, and, with them, the same system of dissociated or hyper aroused response. In turn, a child will often seek to heal those wounds, understanding that their own sense of safety is dependent upon the parent's ability to process and heal. When the child's intrinsic qualities—those easily manipulated instincts of trust, loyalty, dependency, and bonding—are used to meet the unresolved woundedness of the caregiver, the child becomes the caretaker. They are no longer being honored as the child, but, rather, are saddled with the responsibilities and demands of the adult.

This emotional incest can take place both covertly and overtly, occurring whenever a child's emotional, physical, sexual, or mental boundaries have been crossed. Though many may experience an overt form wherein actual physical or sexual touching takes place, most of the clients Michelle and I treat have experienced covert incest wherein a child is asked to play an inappropriate role in the life of the parent. This role can be cast for a number of reasons—due to the caregiver's own process or substance abuse, by creating a unique or favorite child dynamic, by establishing an unhealthy level of emotional intimacy between parent and child or by failing to respect the unique qualities, boundaries, and rights of the child.

The child is accustomed to helping the caregiver regulate his or her own emotions, being asked to play such roles as partner, nurse, protector, or defender. Though unconditional love should flow from parent to child, the parent seeks the same level of unconditional care from the child, providing the stable and secure foundation for the parent rather than vice versa. As the child begins to form relationships outside the family system, they mirror this behavior. As adults, we often repeat the same violations done unto us as children, passing down this pattern of unhealthy relational attachment.

Sadly, we are not often aware when we are crossing these lines. Trapped in the old belief system, we cannot create emotional harmony either in our own choices or in the way we attach to others. We think by asserting control we are expressing love. We try to adjust our behaviors to fit other's expectations of us, even if they are incongruent with our own ideals and belief systems. We believe that by complying with another's demands, we are connecting, but, really, we are just experiencing an inauthentic communication between one's expressed desires and another's adapted behavior. Instead of two healthy people attaching in an emotionally coherent manner, they become addicted to the relationship, just as their caregivers were addicted to them.

About a year into Cathy's work in group therapy, she went to the Reconstruction of one of her fellow members, Tracy. While there, Cathy was asked to participate in a family sculpt wherein the group enacted various members of Tracy's family, illustrating the relational template in which she was raised. Though Tracy had never expressed any grievances against Cathy, when Cathy was asked to sculpt the role of one of Tracy's siblings, a younger sister she loved dearly, Tracy took one look at Cathy, and said, "No, she can't play my sister."

Cathy was distraught. A couple of weeks later, she called the woman and asked why. Tracy explained, "I guess when I hear about your relationship with your children, how depressed and removed you have always felt from their lives and how absorbed you were in your love addiction, you just remind me too much of my mother."

The woman Tracy described didn't sound like what Cathy thought of herself. Instead, Cathy was struck by how much the description resembled her own mother. Cathy realized, "I have become my depressed mother."

Though Cathy still maintained a vision of herself that was connected to her Authentic Self, that creative, sweet, light-hearted child, she had transformed into an unrecognizable Adaptable Self, modeled on the one person she never wanted nor believed she would become: her mother.

Unfortunately, unrepaired trauma gives us very little choice in these behavioral patterns, as we are neurologically wired to react and respond to developmental or shock trauma based on the reactions and responses of our caregivers, either reflecting healthy attachment or the trauma bonds in which we were raised. This is what SomEx^{SM} aims to resolve. By creating repair around the woundedness of our childhoods, we begin to expand that zone in which we can properly process emotional events, creating flexibility and resilience in how we manage our reactions to, and our relationships with, the world around us. We are able to create choice making around who we attach to and how we negotiate that attachment, finally learning how to make healthy relationships. The best part? We don't have to be our depressed mothers anymore.

BRAIN BASICS BY MICHELLE – AUTONOMIC NERVOUS SYSTEM

The Autonomic Nervous System is our brain's first line of interaction between our internal and external worlds. Before we are even cognizant of it, our Autonomic Nervous System is busy assessing and processing all the elements of our environment. Derived from the oldest parts of our brain, the Autonomic Nervous System helps us in our ability to react and respond to the world at large. Not only does it help us to understand that the day is hot or that water is wet, it also helps us to survive by detecting threat in our environment and by sending signals to the body to help us fight, flight, or freeze in order to escape potential danger. Much of this information is taken in through neuroception, which is the body's ability to take in cues from the environment in order to help us sense danger or safety. This may be the elusive "sixth sense" – our intuitive ability to pick up information in a non-linear, cognitive way. Whether in the body of a human or animal, the Autonomic Nervous System creates the same response to threat and trauma, fighting and fleeing when possible, and ultimately freezing into dissociated collapse when response is futile.

Spinal Nerves – Note position of dorsal root ganglion

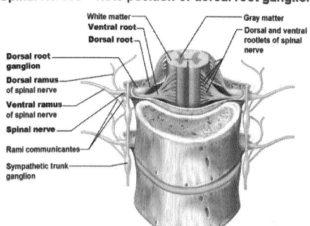

The autonomic nervous system, which manages the unconscious aspects of the body, is made up of two systems: the sympathetic nervous system, which is responsible for the fight or flight response in the body, and the parasympathetic nervous system. Most of the time, these systems compliment each other, unless the fight or flight response is triggered.

The parasympathetic system is guided by the vagus nerve, which runs throughout the body. The vagus nerve has two parts: the ventral vagal, or smart nerve, and the dorsal vagal, otherwise known as the dumb nerve. The ventral vagal has a thick myelin sheath, which helps the speed and ability with which a nerve is able to carry messages throughout the body. Unsurprisingly, the ventral vagal is connected to everything above the diaphragm—face, throat, larynx, lungs, and heart—which are responsible for our immediate responses to the world around us. Most importantly, it is these elements that facilitate social engagement with others, allowing us to determine all those intricate and often intuitive forms of communication—prosody, pitch, tone, and facial expressions—so that we can react appropriately. It is the part of our brain that tells us to smile when someone appears friendly or to divert our attention when we feel fear.

The other part of the vagus nerve is the dorsal vagal, or, as it is often called, "the dumb nerve." It is involved in digestion, sexual response, deep relaxation, release of opiates, and preparation for death. It's the one that comes online to bring the elevator down, attempting to restore the autonomic system to a place where it can begin to repair, or to surrender when escape is impossible.

These key pieces of the autonomic nervous system help us decipher the external world, prompting us to act accordingly. When in a state of safety, the ventral vagal comes online. We express our safety through the expression of social engagement. We are able to make eye contact, our breath is regulated, our pupils are moderate, and our skin warm and dry. We smile, our eyes soften, and our cheeks and jaw relax. We are able to calmly comprehend and communicate with our environment.

However, imagine a person is in a very different situation. Instead of participating in a safe and friendly engagement with the world, he is running for his life. He will become sympathetically aroused in a state of fight, flight, or freeze. He tries to orient with his surroundings, looking for a safe place to hide, his digestion slowing in an attempt to conserve energy. The man realizes that he will not outrun the predator nor is there a place for him to hide or escape. Knowing that neither fight nor flight will save him, his dorsal vagal comes on line, causing him to freeze or dissociate. When humans are in this state, they cannot engage that part of the parasympathetic system that is responsible for the ventral vagal response. Therefore they cannot attune to anyone else around them, they can only focus on the threat.

It can be even more damaging when it is a child who fears a parent's physical or even verbal abuse. He or she will not be able to focus on outside elements (school, socializing, or engaging with others), focusing instead on the source of their threat. This constant state of sympathetic arousal coupled with an attempt to be engaged (after all, it is their parent) develops an organization in the body for attachment in this way. This may follow into adulthood as they attach in relationships which keep them in a constant state of sympathetic arousal.

As for the person running for their life, eventually, once they realize they cannot fight or flee, they will prepare to die, falling into despair, anguish, and hopelessness, their digestion and circulation dropping into a freeze. The same is no different for the terrified child who is unable to fight or leave; however, in such emotionally-triggered states of fear, the experiences of despair and dissociation may not be so obvious.

When escape or fight is futile and despair sets in, the Autonomic Nervous System goes into the freeze state. The best description is like hitting the break and the gas at the same time. The activation is so high it overwhelms the body, forcing it into a collapsed state. This state is called freeze but contains tremendous sympathetic energy. When this energy is not discharged, and, rather, is held in the body, the long-term effects can be devastating.

This is often seen in animals that live in the wild and are faced with predatory activity everyday. Studies have shown that after a gazelle has survived a predator's attack, normally running and fleeing for many hours to survive, they will find a thicket in which to hide, discharging any held energy from the escape. As their body naturally releases that energy through trembling, panting, and at times losing control of bladder and bowels, the gazelle will come back to a regulated state in the Autonomic Nervous System. This repair can take hours or days; there are times when the animal cannot repair and collapses into death.

For those raised in abusive or emotionally dis-regulated homes, they were never given a safe thicket in which to find repair. Instead, they lived in the thwarted response of their own nervous systems, unable to regulate, they dissociated from life. Either that, or they tried to achieve a sense of aliveness by overcompensating in their behaviors. This is where addiction comes in. When one is raised in dorsal vagal collapse, they either succumb to hopelessness and depression, or they find ways to self-soothe. They have adapted to such a high arousal environment that they can only feel the most intense of stimuli. It is as though they are living in a rubber suit: they can't feel a match, but they can feel a blowtorch. It is why so many addicts say that they use the substances and processes to help them feel normal.

In learning how to regulate our emotions, we are able to maintain connection in the ventral vagal state, which allows us to assess and respond to our environment, facilitating social engagement and interpersonal consciousness. Instead of retreating into addiction or the Adaptable Self, which normalizes the trauma, we are able to respond to life in a coherent, harmonious way, creating secure attachments with those around us and creating safety for those who attach to us.

CHAPTER THREE

Attention and Intention

According to neuroscientist and writer Dan Siegel, there are five strategies for changing the brain: attention, trust, memory modification, the unlearning and re-regulation of behavioral patterns, and the process of deep practice. In terms of somatic experiential therapies, we call the first of these Somatic Attention, meaning that we start to change our brains by paying attention to our bodies.

Though it's a rare day when I actually hear the words out of a client's mouth, there are many times where everything about their posture, their choices, their behaviors and attitudes say, "I don't want to change!" And I don't blame them. Change is hard, and it takes work. Change demands that we relinquish old concepts and ways of believing and behaving. Change requires that we rewire our brains, and more often than not, we are afraid of what that change might bring. *What* will we have to let go of? *Who* will we have to let go of? *How* will we be able to negotiate the world without those belief systems that have been passed down for generations?

Though every successful therapeutic effort over the last 150 years has essentially promoted this process, including twelve step and behavioral modification modalities, only in the past ten years have we begun to understand the real science behind it. For many folks who come into therapy, they are entering with one form of an addiction or another—food, love, sex, drugs (and this includes prescription medication), alcohol, relationships, debting, spending, and more. Unfortunately, most addicts function within a narrow arousal zone. They are only able to override its constrictions by keeping themselves medicated. Addiction is not an integrated experience. It is a form of pseudo-individuation where the addict is forced to step outside their Authentic Self and operate outside their internal value system in order to function in their addiction. They are living in a double bind in which they attempt to separate themselves from the dysfunctions of the family system, yet the addiction exacerbates the effects of it. They get caught in the contradictory messages of their own behavior—"I'm functioning but not feeling."

This process is as much a neurological state as it is an emotional one. For many addicts, the mind has become isolated from the body or parts of the body, often resulting in the present lived experience being obscured by the unresolved affects of the past. Our biography once again becomes our biology. But integration is possible, and it is where real change takes place.

As we begin to explore and re-negotiate the experience of our biography, we have the potential to affect our biology. But before we can engage this process of refocusing our reactions to old life stories, we must first become attuned to the world around us and our behaviors. This is why only through deep practice this attunement can become a way of life. The more you become attentive to your choices and create intention around them, the more myelinated the nerve pathway will become, allowing for the message to travel faster. If instead of moving into rage, one is able to better resource and regulate their emotions, they will create a neural pathway for a new behavior. The more they practice the behavior, the more myelinated the neural pathway, and the faster the new behavior will take place. For those who have done any kind of twelve-step work, this concept is embodied in the idea of ninety meetings in ninety days. First, we must become attentive to our behaviors, then we must create intention for creating new ones, slowly training those neurons to both wire and fire together in new patterns.

This is why this process takes place in stages, and there has to be a period of abstinence and/or moderation from addiction in order to create a safe and recovered foundation from which to venture into this deeper work. It might sound like a long road at the outset, but such change can and does occur. I see it everyday. As I have said before, one of the most critical pieces of this work is social engagement with a therapist or therapeutic community. As a facilitator of this process, I create individualized therapeutic plans for my clients while intentionally building safety and coherence between other resources, including the therapeutic process itself. Through various modalities, including group therapy, people are able to go deeper into their issues and expand their capacity to tolerate a wider range of emotions thus expanding their Optimal Arousal Zone. In order to see those same benefits, I implore you to find a similar space within your own community by finding a therapist who practices either somatic or experiential work and who can walk with you along this road to change.

"You keep pushing and pushing and pushing until I scream"

The word somatic means "of the body or relating to the body." When we begin to have somatic attention, we are creating a form of consciousness that begins with voluntary intention to focus attention within the body. Classic psychotherapy is about focusing on the problem, but in SomEx^{SM}, we focus more on what is resourceful than what is traumatic. Because no matter what might have happened in the past, it is actually the body's inclination to develop resiliency to stress that allows us to heal. It is why children bounce back so quickly from falling down or getting hurt. Our bodies were built to rebound. The goal of somatic therapy is to return the body to that natural state of resiliency, repairing those attachment disorders and relational trauma that keep it working outside of the Optimal Arousal Zone and restoring it to its harmonious center. But when we live outside that center, we try to find things to help us self-regulate. Now, I have seen every form of addiction there is, but love addiction is still the most potent addiction I treat.

When Cathy came to me, all she wanted to talk about was Chris and Bill. Her world had been focused on the men in her life for so long, there was little left of her. She was distraught, and she was willing to do anything. She could not let go of Chris no matter how hard she tried. In a letter she wrote to him but never sent, she explained, "You promised me a different life. You promised I would now be safe. You said that I would never have any reason to distrust you and then, just when I finally believed all your promises, I find out you're no different. You're just a better liar. And then you call me crazy and ungrateful and 'entitled.' You keep pushing and pushing until I scream. I hate your promises. I hate that you make me doubt myself and the whole world around me. I am not crazy. You make me CRAZY."

Crazy is not a word we like to use around here, but if you use Einstein's famous definition of insanity as doing something over and over and expecting a different result, well, then, crazy Cathy was. She lived in either the hyper aroused, "pushing until I scream" place or the dissociated, "please touch me so I can feel something" place, and neither took place in the Optimal Arousal Zone.

In order to begin rewiring and refiring those neurons, she first had to be able to find that calm and resourced center from which the work could begin. Since Cathy lived in either an experience of intense danger, as she had learned as a child and in her sexual relationships with Bill (engaging the sympathetic nervous system), or within the passive collapse of one who is experiencing a life threat (engaging the parasympathetic), she didn't know how to respond to Chris' betrayal with anything but that twisted combination of scream and freeze. The gas and the brakes were both punched in. "Crazy" could be the only result. Our goal was to get her into the middle, the ventral vagal safety zone, the optimal arousal state for processing life.

By drawing attention to somatic indicators, such as the sound of her breath, the feeling of her feet against the floor, her palms placed upon her lap, we were able to start working through those pieces of Chris, Bill, and her entire life, which had led to such a constricted breadth of emotional processing. Like most children raised in households where one parent lives in volatile arousal and the other is shut down and avoidant, Cathy had become an emotional bulimic, restricting and then binging on her own responsive behaviors. By creating an environment of safety, compassion, and trust, I was able to help her attend to somatic indicators, such as her breath, fluctuations in temperature, energetic vibrations, and other markers. We began to cultivate and nurture her attention to these indicators so we could begin to expand her somatic attention.

Even for myself, I find that whenever I have trouble regulating myself, it is the breath that is first to re-center me. With Cathy, we started with some simple guided meditations, allowing her to focus on something other than Chris. As she engaged in these guided exercises, Cathy was better able to discern her own inner subjective experience. At first, those realizations came in fits and starts—"I'm angry," "I'm hot," "There's a fly in the room"—but over time Cathy's breadth of perception began to grow, and we started expanding her awareness, observing other sensations and dissociated parts. Another tool in somatic attention is to use oscillating attention between polarities, such as constricted versus relaxed, light versus dense, and pleasant versus uncomfortable.

As Don Johnson, a pioneer in the field of experiential science, explains in *The Body in Psychotherapy*, this "clear articulation of experiential knowing is demanding and requires long education in the practice of awareness." Slowly, Cathy began to observe subtle sensations, and through that practice, her awareness of her body began to return.

Various modalities of energy and bodywork help to facilitate the process of attention to somatic experiences. Listed below are three main areas of benefit for clients receiving this type of work:

- Safe touch – Many clients with a complex attachment or trauma history are touch deprived, touch defensive, or can only experience touch through a sexual lens. Receiving safe touch can restore a client's ability to have pleasant embodied experiences, re-build trust, and provide resources to enable deeper re-integration of the whole self.

- Direct attention to chronic tensions – Over time, our bodies create soft tissue tension patterns in the effort to habitually express or repress feelings, actions, or beliefs. All hands-on therapies have the potential to bring awareness and the process of change to these conscious and unconscious patterns. This process can also help the body re-educate and remember long-forgotten healthy patterns. A skilled practitioner can utilize techniques that are still or active, silent or verbal, physiologically or energetically based to customize an approach that is safe and effective for exploring deeply held bodymind (or somatic) patterns. At EHC we utilize practitioners who are trained in multiple bodywork modalities (including Fascial Freedom Technique, Jin Shin Do® Bodymind Acupressure, CranioSacral Therapy, etc.) and who are able to utilize verbal communication to provide this unique form of bodymind [somatic] therapy.

• Deep relaxation and regulation – When doing intensive Somatic Experiential Therapies, it is also important to provide soothing, comforting, deepening, and regulating hands-on work. Through traditional modalities such as Swedish massage and Reiki, clients are able to receive the wonderful benefits of deep relaxation and supportive, safe touch. If so much of our dis-regulation or addictive behaviors have root in an inability to be fully embodied, these therapies can provide regulated, relaxed, safe embodiment opportunities.

Hands-on bodywork is an integrating, soothing, comforting, and necessary interlude within the more intensive SomEx℠ process. It can be the necessary therapeutic intervention that provides key insights, awareness, or a breakthrough that truly deepens and enhances the entire process.

As Cathy found out, sometimes all it takes is a massage to set a part of ourselves free. A couple of years back, she was having a traditional massage. After the session, when the therapist placed two fingers on Cathy's ankle and two on her wrist, as they do in Jin Shin Do, a style of acupressure, Cathy had one of the most eye-opening experiences of her life. She told me later, "It was the first time I had experienced feeling my entire body at the same time."

Slowly, through these various methods, we were able to tweeze apart her obsessive attention to Chris and, in an embodied way, bring the attention to herself. Though, consciously, Cathy was having the experience of finally attending to her own body, subconsciously, her neurons had been working to create a new neural pathway. By methodically and gently attending to herself, she began to understand ways in which her body responded to the present moment and simultaneously began to appreciate the ways in which she had coped with past traumas. According to Australian psychiatrist Russell Meares, who writes in *The Metaphor of Play*, this process leads to "the recovery of 'aliveness' by means of bodily feelings which underlie it and which are the foundations upon which a personal reality is based."

Cathy told me later, "After that day, I would have these experiences of pushing a grocery cart, where I could feel my hands, and the air against my face and my body moving forward. For the first time, I was restored back to my body."

When we begin to have somatic awareness, our attention moves to the phenomena of the present moment. As leading neuroscientist Christof Koch writes in *The Quest for Consciousness*, "Coalitions of nerve cells form, dissolve and reform continually, weaving our ever-changing but integral sense of consciousness. When two neurons that are far apart become synchronized, they do so in an oscillatory fashion." And so, through the oscillating practice of bringing Cathy's attention to the world around her, we were able to focus on the present moment, and Cathy began to take her first real step towards change: she began to pay attention to herself.

"I resent that you used my childhood molestation as a weapon"

As Wendy Maltz writes in *The Sexual Healing Journey*, "Sexual healing is a dynamic process. We gain understanding about how our sexuality has been affected by sexual abuse, make changes in our sexual attitudes and behaviors, and develop new skills for experiencing sex in a positive way. One type of change encourages another."

For Cathy, her sexuality had been adversely affected long before Bill, or certainly Chris, showed up. When I saw what Cathy had written about her childhood molestation, I was filled with compassion for how this woman and her sexuality had been affected by the abuse. It was short, but those nine lines had become part of the sexual/relational template that she had brought into her adult life:

> *I go to visit Mr. Jackson in his basement. I have been there many times. He has fish tanks down there, and we go to see the fish. He puts his arm around me. He puts his hand down the front of my pants and touches me. His hand is trembling and he touches very lightly. He asks if I know what that is. I tell him, "Julie says it's a cunt." He laughs.*

That laughter created a coupling for Cathy, which fused sexual violation with shame—a behavioral pattern that sustained much of her relationship with Bill and helped to quickly escalate the abuse in her relationship with Chris. For Cathy, these early events became the blueprint for her activation in her sexual/relational template. A fixed action pattern is significant in animal behavior because it represents the simplest type of behavior in which a readily defined stimulus nearly always results in an invariable behavioral response. For Cathy, the mere mention of her assault brings on a hypo sexual freeze state.

Fixed action patterns were first detected in the behavioral patterns of animals. What became increasingly interesting to researchers was to see how certain breeds would actually exploit the patterns of another breed to their own ends. A well-known example of this is brood parasitism in which one species will lay its eggs in the nest of another species, which will then parent its young. Because it is working off its own fixed action patterns of hunting for enough food to meet the needs of it young, the smaller bird will work extra hard in order to find enough food for the other species as well as their own, trapped in the fixed action patterns their survival demands.

To a certain extent, Bill took advantage of a similar vulnerability. Recognizing Cathy's own natural reaction to sexual trauma, he was able to exploit the pattern to meet the needs of his addiction. Later in Cathy's therapy, she writes him a letter, explaining all the reasons why she resents her first husband. On the list is the charge: "I resent that you used my childhood molestation as a weapon to get me to perform for you sexually."

Once she met Chris, Cathy was utterly incapable of recognizing the same patterns within their relationship. In fact, she was quickly telling her sisters that she had found her "knight in shining armor." But the romantic overtures were just another form of grooming, another re-enactment of her childhood trauma where an easy joke was supposed to make light of the grossest of indiscretions.

For many of us, these fixed action patterns guide our behaviors and responses. We live in the idea that we are what was done to us, creating an addictive template out of these re-enactments of our trauma. For Cathy, what started as an attachment disorder became co-sex addiction. According to Stephanie Carnes in *Mending a Shattered Heart*, some of the characteristics of co-sex addiction include:

- Denial – Carnes describes this infamous process: "Co-addicts commonly find themselves believing tall tales or far-fetched explanations." So often my clients come in defending the loved one that is harming them, believing the lie because they have been raised to believe the lie.
- Preoccupation – The co-sex addict will become preoccupied with the sex addict and their behaviors, allowing it to be the focus of their lives.
- Enabling/Rescuing – The co-sex addict will make excuses and try to rescue and protect the sex addict even at the risk of their own safety or happiness.

- Taking excessive responsibility – Twelve step groups often say, "You didn't cause it, you can't cure it, and you can't control it," but the co-sex addict often believes that they have done and can do all three.

- Emotional turmoil – The co-sex addict lives on the roller coaster of the other person's addictions. They are often caught between trying to keep up appearances on the outside and suffering the consequences of the addiction on the inside.

- Efforts to control – According to Carnes, "Many co-addicts find themselves thinking, 'If the addict would just do _____, everything would fall into place.'" The co-sex addict believes that if only they were in charge of the addict's choices, their behaviors might be different.

- Compromise of self – The co-sex addict often cannot exist within the reality of the addict and is forced to adapt, living out of the compromise and negotiation of their Adaptable Self, and losing their Authentic Self in the mix.

- Anger – Understandably, the co-sex addict experiences great anger at the choices and behavior of their partner. However, they may choose to express this anger either overtly—through excessive rage and even violence—or covertly—through passive aggressive behaviors.

- Sexual issues – As Carnes explains, "Since these relationships often contain more than one sexual abuse victim, naturally there are higher rates of sexual issues with these coupleships." As I have seen with my own clients, sexual bulimia or anorexia often goes hand in hand with co-sex addiction, for both parties.

For many people who live in sex, love, or co-addiction, isolation is one of the symptoms of their disorder. We have found at EHC that the best way to invite people out of their isolation is through group therapies. In doing experiential work, we are attempting to make the implicit memory accessible to the explicit awareness. By using methods that enhance the sensory experience and make it more vivid, we attempt to help transform the unresolved trauma into a harmonious state through the empathy of shared experience.

In order to begin to re-negotiate Cathy's trauma, we started oscillating between a soothing resource and the compartmentalized pain from her past. Thankfully, Cathy was in group therapy at the time, which allowed us to utilize the group and methods to explore her traumas. By bringing in that sensory awareness that, by now, Cathy was well practiced in, we were able to incorporate these disassociated parts and to start repairing the attachment traumas from her childhood. This work must be done with careful and cautious preparation wherein both the therapist and client work towards regulating and integrating the experience.

In order to be restored to our Optimal Arousal Zones, we must first trust the environment and social engagement we are participating in. Cathy had to get to know and trust the other clients in the group. She had to begin to feel empathy for them—and they for her—before we could start working through some of the feelings around her molestation. We moved through the experience with slow, deliberate oscillations, keeping Cathy grounded in her process throughout. We would use such techniques as centering ("Can you feel your feet against the ground? Do you feel your hands?"), restoring rhythm ("Breathe in. Hold your breath for a moment, and breath out."), and orienting ("Look around the room, Cathy, and make some eye contact"). Through these processes, we would create awareness in her present space, and keep her grounded, centered, and oriented within her Optimal Arousal Zone.

Just as Cathy had developed the fixed action patterns to freeze when confronted with trauma, she now had to build new patterns, ones that would allow her to find her Optimal Arousal Zone even while re-negotiating the trauma. We would begin by bringing in a symbol of her inner child, as enacted by one of her group partners. In Psychodrama, this is what is known as the double, as it allows the client to explore what was unsaid and unprocessed in the moment. As Tian Dayton explains in *The Living Stage*, "The double speaks the inner life of the protagonist (the primary client in the exercise), bringing the material that is lodged in the background toward the foreground."

The inner child role player told Cathy how Mr. Jackson made her feel ("I'm scared. I want to go home. Why won't anyone protect me?"). One of the other group members played Mr. Jackson who stood across the room laughing at her. At first, Cathy froze, unable to protect her inner child symbol and unable to speak out against her abuser, but as the inner child symbol continued to beg her for the protection Cathy's own parents failed to offer, something in Cathy began to shift.

I worked with her, asking her to tell me if she noticed her feet and how they were connected to the floor, to focus on her breathing, and, slowly, as Cathy found her voice, finally standing between the inner child symbol and her perpetrator, she demanded that the group member roleplaying "Mr. Jackson" stop laughing.

"It's not funny," she shouted, finding her voice.

I coached her as her inner child role player cheered her on. "Try and stay present here Cathy," I suggested. "Say what you need to say but stay here."

Cathy looked across the room into the eyes of the group member playing her perpetrator, and said slowly and calmly, "It's not funny."

Slowly, we oscillated between the hyper, sympathetic arousal state, and the resource of a safe group member to connect her to a safe, relational resource. Similarly, as we would move through pieces around Bill and Chris, she began to experience emotional freeze or numbing, her back going stiff, her eyes shifting downward. We would continue to resource, ground and center her during the moments of activation. I would ask her to breathe, to feel the air against her face, the ground beneath her feet, and she would come back to her Optimal Arousal Zone, breathing clearly, her heart rate would slow, and her pupils would contract. She would come back to life.

Over time, we began to change the memory of the trauma. As Russell Meares writes in the *Metaphor of Play*, "[trauma] must be transformed from a sudden, almost instantaneous distress which slices into, and has no connection with, the experiences of everyday living, into an experience which can be integrated into the larger consciousness of self, including its past or memories and future perspectives."

Addicts relapse more around success than they do failure because they have such a constricted arousal zone. They have no flexibility around their emotions—great depression and great joy can both lead them out of their Optimal Arousal Zone. That's why, when we do this work, I want my clients to be in a well-supported, resourced, and regulated place. From there, they can begin to incorporate those parts that they previously found intolerable into their Optimal Arousal Zone. They begin to find resiliency around their emotions and behaviors, creating a wider range of flexibility around their ability to process life.

You can't touch the sweet without touching the bitter, yet, at the same time, it is pertinent that the journeys into both are grounded and conducted in a safe relationship or community. When we are in a state of sympathetic or hyper arousal, it "creates a chain of events that results in attempts to engage, defend, and aggress." These indicators include:

- Increased force of cardiac contraction leading to cold pale skin
- Dilated pupils wherein the whites of the eyes are highly visible

- The secretion of saliva is inhibited making the mouth feels dry
- Heart rate is accelerated
- Adrenaline is stimulated
- Gastro-intestinal activity is inhibited

When people experience intense danger as children, as Cathy did at the hands of her father, they will feel the experience of fight, flight, or freeze. Much like the polar bear in the video, these basic instinctual responses take place when there is over-activation of the autonomic nervous system. What will ultimately start with fight or flight will ultimately end in the collapse of freeze, unless the trauma is resolved and repaired.

Likewise, if one is not able to make sense of a life experience—as Cathy was unable to do because of her neighbor's molestation, or to a much lesser degree, as the infant in the still face video—they will fall into collapse, experiencing avoidance, numbing, emotional constriction, detachment and dissociation.

Indicators of the dorsal vagal tone are:

- Core systems of respiration, circulation, and digestion are slowed down
- Extreme dorsal vagal tone is experienced at times of trauma as a way to avoid detection, i.e. playing possum
- Attempts to defend by fighting or physically fleeing are not perceived as options
- Aspects of respiration, digestion and/or circulation drop into a freeze response
- Emotions of despair, anguish, hopelessness and helplessness coexist with states of depression and dissociation

Cathy lived in this state for much of her marriage to Bill. She spent days hiding from her husband's sexual advances, unable to say no and yet finding that when she did, her words did little to stop the chronic abuse that was part of their marriage. She had lost all physical and sexual boundaries with this man, and her trauma bond was like a collar around her neck. Yet, at the same time, she found herself overcome by rage and emotion. When her son was nine years old, she once slapped him across the face, adrenaline coursing through her. The same violence that had once boiled up in her father now boiled up in her. As Sharon Stanley explains, "the memory of the original reaction to the traumatic event is retained in the implicit memory system of the right hemisphere of the brain. The amygdala is continually searching for reminders in the present moment of the original trauma so that it feels prepared to survive."

In trauma, the sympathetic, or hyper, arousal state propels one to aggress, defend, and protect. As Michelle explains, there is so much sympathetic arousal that a switch gets flipped and the dorsal vagal, or hypo, state of immobility simultaneously comes on line. All that energy is still in the body when you have the collapse, and if you don't have a way to discharge the thwarted energy, it can become depression and anxiety. It was this coupling pattern that had caught Cathy in its traumatic grip her whole life, trapped between the chronic violence of her father and her inevitable collapse. In that neurological confusion, Cathy lost all identity.

I know that though my childhood was not marred by such abuse, my lack of proper attachment also led me to live in an Adaptable Self, which believed that as long as I was pleasing my mother, I was being my best self. When I was in high school and started fooling around with other male friends, I didn't even know what that meant. There was one high school teacher who was rumored to be a "queer" and all I knew was that you didn't want to be him. I was so disconnected from myself, I didn't even realize that was what I was. I was dating a girl in high school for two years before she broke up with me, and all I remember was that I was propelled from a numb state of denial into a profound desire to get drunk. In a way, I did become more aware but not in any sort of integrated way—it was more like I was resigned to the knowledge that, "This isn't something that's going to pass; it's going to be with me for a while." My capacity for experiencing life was so narrow that any awareness of who I really was would quickly thrust me into a place of wanting to numb or run. I knew no in between.

"It's nice when I look in my eyes and know that I'm all mine!"

In order to break this binding between the hyper and hypo-aroused states, another aspect of the work must be introduced. We must begin to tweeze apart the hyper and hypo aroused states by first approaching the effects of trauma as though they are drips of water in a lake of soothing resources. By resourcing the safe, calming elements of one's experience—smells, sights, sounds, movements, imagery, amongst others—these allow for an inner connection to one's strengths and abilities, returning him or her to a sense of purpose and meaning.

Then we are able to resource those elements as we oscillate between the sympathetic and parasympathetic states, staying attentive to the ventral vagal resource of social engagement. In Cathy's autobiography, the stories of her grandmother and grandfather stood out—the only representation of kindness and security she found. In one of those stories was perhaps the greatest resource we could have asked for: a song.

> *We are at Grandma and Grandpa's house. Aunt Gina had a baby and they just got home from the hospital. I am sick and I might get the baby sick, so I can't go. Grandma will stay home with me and go see the baby another time. When everyone leaves, I cry. Grandma tells me the story of when I was born. She says that*

> *Mom and Dad told them that she could give me my*
> *middle name. She told them to name me Cathy May.*
> *When Dad came home he told her, 'We gave her the*
> *middle name you wanted! We named her Cathy Rae!'*
> *My Grandma chortles: 'They must have misunderstood*
> *but, oh well, what do you do? I couldn't ask them to*
> *change the birth certificate.' She tells me I am special*
> *to her, and always have been. She teaches me a song:*
>
> *I love me! I love me!*
> *I'm wild about myself.*
> *I love me! I love me!*
> *My pictures on my shelf.*
> *You may not think*
> *That I'm so grand*
> *But me thinks I'm just fine!*
> *It's nice when I*
> *Look in my eyes*
> *And know that I'm all mine!*

In most of our sculpting work at EHC, I employ music to help people resource. I often ask my clients to create a playlist of music that speaks to them in some way. We then bring that music in as it benefits them during their somatic, experiential work. For Cathy, we had her own song, and what perfection it was. Often I would call in this image of her grandmother, the kindness and care she experienced in her embrace. She would later tell me that the only little shred of self-esteem she had was from her grandmother and those lyrics she never forgot, "It's nice when I look in my eyes and know that I'm all mine!"

Before people can begin re-negotiating on behalf of their authentic selves, they need to first build a connection to that self. They need to resource the safety within before they can establish safe and secure attachments outside of themselves. For Cathy, this memory of her grandmother was the goal of her journey: to move out of the place of love addiction and into a place of self-love. During one of her sculpts, Cathy asked one of her group members to play Bill and another to play Chris. Together they taunted Cathy, saying, "You aren't worth anything! You don't deserve love. You aren't worth a damn!"

For a moment, the abusive messages created a need for her to begin to shut down internally. I began to use resourcing techniques to have her pay more attention to her breath, her body, and herself than to the voices coming from outside herself. As the voices continued, Cathy was able to say some things long held in her body.

She looked at her feet and whispered, "I'm not worth it. I've never been worth it."

As the words came out, she began sobbing at the part of herself that believed the lie. I looked at her and shook my head with compassion, "Oh Cathy." There was no way *not* to feel for her. Not to feel for all of us when we finally say the words that have been haunting us for so long. I looked over to the client who was playing her grandmother and we began to sing, "*I love me! I love me! I'm wild about myself. I love me! I love me! My pictures on my shelf.*"

Cathy began to smile. And then she began to sing with us, and out of the darkness of her dissociation, she began to climb back into her Optimal Arousal Zone. She began to believe a new set of words as we helped re-establish her worth, connecting her back to the values given to her by her grandmother.

"I was present the whole time"

When we do Reconstruction Days, we use the event primarily to address themes and patterns that we have already identified through the therapeutic process. We always begin the resourcing as it provides stabilization for traumatized individuals and the foundation for processing trauma states. And then we begin to build, growing out of the resourcing and into the amplification of the story. Over the course of the exercise, they begin to tolerate the feelings and sensations of their dissociated memories. By strengthening the ventral vagal tone, primarily our ability to assess and appropriately respond to the environment around us, we are able to heal the neural coalitions formed by past trauma. By re-negotiating the somatic experience of an event, we are able to have a neurological transformation of the experience. Resourcing allows us to practice this re-negotiation and repair. Just as in music, harmony is the simultaneous use of various pitches and chords, so in the reconstruction process, we move through these vacillating states of emotional arousal, until, much like the tuning of a piano, the tone is clear and resonant.

When we resource, we are creating a moment of light and strength, but more than that, we are asking that the client stay present and curious in their work. In Cathy's reconstruction process, I was able to ask her, "What is happening in this moment?" And she was able to guide me. I would inquire and empathize, empathize and inquire. I would ask her how she felt, but just as important, I was also *attuned* to those feelings, able to provide an authentic, empathetic, and regulated response to her emotional activation. Unlike in the emotionally dis-regulated family system where pain is ignored or incurred, in resourcing we honor the ways in which the client has found skills to survive. I offered my empathy to Cathy and let her know that what she had experienced was traumatic. It deserved her tears and her pain. I asked for others in the group who have experienced similar trauma to join Cathy. They were able to support her process through their own attentiveness. Just as they were better attuned to their own emotional responses, so they were able to attune to Cathy's, creating the interpersonal consciousness in which healing can begin.

Then I was able to ask, "When you experienced this trauma, what helped you survive? Where do you notice your smile? What has helped you to persevere?" Slowly, Cathy began to engage, coming out of her trauma, reconnecting to her present state of being.

Resources can be drawn from any number of places, including:

- Relational – friends, family members, even pets
- Environmental – elements of nature such as the ocean, the mountains, the wind against one's face
- Spiritual – the presence of God, the Spirit of the Universe, Jesus, Buddha, Allah, Muhammad, Krishna, or any other numbers of Gods or spiritual advisors
- Sensory – the sound of a car going by, the fan beating overhead, the feel of a soft pillow, or some other fabric or scent or sound that brings calm
- Images – sometimes we will cut out pictures from magazines, finding images that speak to the calming strength that people identify with their ventral vagal state
- Internal Strength – for Cathy this was her grandmother's song, but for others it can be the simple connection with their breath, the place in their heart where feeling lies
- Soothing Movement – sometimes just small exercises, a rotation of the ankle or wrist, a light stretching in the body will connect them back in and remind them of the deep somatic place in which this work is occurring.

When we return to the present, we finally learn to be here now. We are able to experience this beautiful blissful stillness. But perhaps even more miraculous, we are able to appropriately process and respond to life. As they say in twelve-step work, "we intuitively know how to handle things that used to baffle us." The goal is not to be hijacked by our histories, our fixed action patterns, our compulsions and addictions, but, rather, to have awareness of our body and to be attentive to our emotional responses by creating intention around our behaviors and choices. This is the present peace in which addiction simply cannot reign. For Cathy, it was the first moments of release from the power of Chris, and, in great part, from Bill. For me, it was the first moments of release of fearing my true identity. I was physically sober. I had been so for a number of years, but then the chance to be emotionally sober beckoned to me, offering me the safe and stable space to finally sing the song I had been silently humming my whole life. And it's there for you too.

As you begin to find the resources in your life, look at what sensations shift you into that optimal state. Is it music? Is it the memory of a loved one? Is it your concept of God? Go through the list of possible resources and see what sensations are brought up in your body. Create a list of things in your life which resonant not with the adapted self of your traumas and addictions but with that Authentic Self inside.

After Cathy's Reconstruction Day, she told me that it was through resourcing her work, by finding and sensing a place of safety even as we dipped into some of her most difficult life experiences, that she no longer felt the need to escape. "I never left, Kent," she exclaimed. "It was a really big victory for me, because I never left. I never once, the entire day, had that 'out of body, I'm gone' experience. I was present the whole time."

PART TWO

Resiliency

CHAPTER FOUR

Developing Trust

*Bill and I were married in the Baptist Church in 1977.
My grandparents had been a part of the church since
the 1960s and were well known and well loved. I went
around that day on a cloud of little old women who
tended to my every need and told everyone we passed,
"This is Hazel's granddaughter!" We went back to
grandma's for lunch after the wedding, then back up to
the ranch for the reception.*

*We went down to New Orleans for the next few
days. Then we loaded up the presents and some of my
belongings and drove back to Dallas.*

*When we got home, I started looking at the college
catalog to plan my semester, but Bill said, "No. You
won't be going to school." When I argued back, he told
me, "We don't have the money for that and, besides,
women are supposed to stay at home with their children."
I submitted.*

For years, Cathy told this story of her early days with Bill.
Cathy's submission became her cross to bear. She had lived in
its details and its resentments, fostering the notion that the choice
was never hers—that it had been taken away long ago.

And, to a certain extent, Cathy was right. She had lived most of her life, compartmentalizing within the left hemisphere, constantly adapting herself to her environments, and normalizing the abnormal. Because our left hemisphere attempts to make meaning out of life's chaos, it compels us to adapt. It is in our right hemisphere that we are able to utilize intuitive and creative abilities that offer change and choice making. It is what moves us beyond the linear thinking of the left hemisphere and allows for a different interpretation of life events. When the left and right hemispheres are integrated, we are able to synthesize the qualities of both hemispheres into a more powerful expression of ourselves.

The right brain is home to wordless communication—such as colors and images, archetypes and dreams—but when people are asked how they feel, they typically respond with a value judgment that comes from a left-brain analysis. Part of SomEx[SM] is to move them away from the left-hemisphere description of an emotion, and into its sensory experience. The right hemisphere allows us to connect to others' experiences and to expand those interpersonal relationships into a broader community.

A healthy and well-attached therapeutic relationship helps us to move from the left-brain processing of our history into one that is integrated and coherent. It allows us to not only recover the dissociated memories of our stories but to re-negotiate them through a deeper sensory experience. It is through this process that we do more than make meaning out of our past, we create choicefulness for the future.

In the process of integration, it's imperative that we experience a level of empathy around our life story. The left hemisphere teaches us to categorize, to judge, and to rank our life data, whereas the right hemisphere allows us to experience its emotional content. For those of us who came from an emotionally dis-regulated home, we seldom experienced this level of attunement or empathy. When those around you are likewise working from similar left-hemisphere states, there is no way for them not to diminish your experience. The left brain whispers to the right hemisphere, "It's not that bad. Others have had worse." Not surprisingly, these are the same words that are echoed in dysfunctional families: "You think you have it bad" or "You should have seen what it was like for me growing up."

But this process of left-brain dissociation is not without its merits. The left brain is offering a protective mechanism that blocks us from having to process feelings around trauma. By keeping us compartmentalized, it is also protecting us until we are in a safe place with safe people where it can be re-negotiated. As time goes on, however, it also prevents us from stepping into healing. But in order to heal pain, we must first be willing to recognize it. There comes a time when we must highlight the trauma in order to heal it. But we cannot do that alone.

At this point in the work, clients begin to have a greater attunement to their sensory landscape, and, simultaneously, they are better able to attend to the world around them. From there, they can begin to build upon that awareness within a therapeutic effort to experience healthy somatic empathy between themselves and another. This is not just about a quick fix for the isolated problem that drove us to therapy or to seek help. It takes deep commitment to develop healthier relational attachment templates. The good news is that life doesn't start when you're done with this process; it starts when you begin it. You begin to live in the process of healing—finding friendship, and repair and discovering again that playful, loving, passionate being inside.

This is why a therapist's role is not merely to sit and listen to yet another life narrative but to become a resource in its reintegration, to work as a trusted guide. In order to participate in someone else's healing however, the therapist must be willing to look at his or her own story before they can help someone else process theirs. Empathy comes from having walked the healing road, and though all our stories might look different, recovery is a shared experience. When a therapist can look at their client and say, "I get what you're saying," and mean it from that genuine, somatically integrated, emotionally regulated place, they are creating that first bridge towards the Somatic Trust that is necessary for transformation. I don't take my job lightly. I understand that I can't offer what I haven't got, and I also can't substitute anything—including the writing of these chapters—with real human interaction and the chance for interpersonal transformation. No book, lecture, television show, radio program, or quick fix will do. But by finally doing the therapeutic work, we come to the place where we no longer have to numb the pain in order to protect ourselves from the effects of trauma. Instead, we become choice makers in how we are going to heal from it.

"I wasn't going to do this stuff unless I had some immediate results"

I could tell by my first meeting with Cathy that she was hoping I would be able to fix her in one week and send her on her way, like a last minute diet before summer began. She wanted to tell me her stories of Chris—how he hurt her, how she did everything for him, all the promises he made to her, how she wanted to keep the relationship—and then have Chris return. When most clients start therapy, mostly what I hear from them is, "He did this or she does that," but with Cathy, it was different. All she could say was, "I did this for him and I've done that." Finally, I stopped her, and reminded her that partnership is about the "we," not the "I." I asked her, "Cathy, why are you so willing to take responsibility for the coupleship? Both of you have a part in how you've gotten to this place, but this process demands that each person take responsibility for his or her share. Trying to be the hero can be just as messy as being the villain."

She stared at me blankly but made another appointment. For me, resiliency is about perseverance and commitment; it's about the body's ability to tolerate distress and feelings and still show up to deal with what's in front of us. Though Cathy had been submitting to others' demands her whole life, something happened that day that compelled her to commit to herself instead. Some small spark of her Authentic Self came to light and she decided to schedule a second appointment, not knowing until much later just how much courage it took for her to take that initial step on the road towards recovery. Fortunately, many of the traits that she had developed out of her Adaptable Self—her coping mechanisms, her determination not to quit or fail—could actually be used to her benefit in the recovery process.

I suggested she attend one of our upcoming traumatic reparation retreats wherein we apply the principles of SomEx^SM and begin to find integration and repair within a six-day workshop. Though at first she balked, Cathy decided at the last moment to attend. It was here she was first introduced to experiential work. As she told me later, "I remember we were doing a family sculpt, and, though I was watching someone's else's life story being played out, I couldn't help but feel it as my own. I could feel it in my bones; it was as though I had been through the same thing."

Through the course of the week, Cathy's emotional issues began to show up as somaticized stress, the body's way of manifesting unexpressed emotions. Over the first few days, she complained that her wrists hurt, though she hadn't participated in any exercises which would be the cause.

She shared, "My body was just tender from inside, and I decided that I wasn't going to do this stuff unless I had some immediate results." I asked if Cathy was interested in exploring what her body was communicating to her through her somaticized sensations. We started by focusing attention on the parts of her body that didn't feel pain, and then we would oscillate attention into areas where she did experience discomfort, attempting to amplify the sensations that were pain-free. As she began to do that, she experienced an internal shift as she began to open up to the group, telling them how she had always wanted to be a writer. She explained how she had acquiesced that dream in her first marriage, and, as she continued to process the story both somatically and narratively, we tracked what was going on with the pain until she realized that the pain was beginning to dissipate in her wrists.

That story she had told a million times had finally become integrated, moving from the meaning-making left-brain story of "he did this and I did that" into a right brain experience, tracking sensation while attending to the story. She began to see that she didn't have to submit in the way that she had for years, but instead, she could begin to develop those authentic qualities that had been lost in her childhood and marriage. She could begin to heal.

Antonio Damasio writes, "All living organisms are born with devices designed to solve automatically, no proper reasoning required, the basic problems of life." This right-brain structure was created to fend "off external agents of disease and physical injury," but when trauma is introduced, the brain must respond by withdrawing and approaching, constricting and expanding in order to defend itself from the external threat. For Cathy, she was so constricted she could not even process emotional pain from an emotional place; instead, it came out through the pain in her wrist.

In order to begin the work back into her right brain, Cathy had to first start connecting to the world around her. Both the left and right hemispheres carry communications about internal thoughts and feelings, attempting to assimilate them into our perception of reality. Both hemispheres share certain processing centers in the nervous system, linking us to our thoughts and the sensory experiences around us. These communications help to interpret, govern, and transmit our reality, creating an interpersonal consciousness between humans.

People are constantly receiving information through both hemispheres because they are constantly assessing their environment. The left brain is determining what the actions and outwards markers (e.g. what people are saying) are displaying while the right hemisphere is picking up on the more intuitive indicators of the environment (e.g. evaluations of another person's energy). Problems arise when those hemispheres don't harmonize, when there is dissonance between what the left hemisphere is encountering and what the right hemisphere is attuning to.

That is when an Adaptable Self emerges, when we must change our behaviors or ideals in order to create a semblance of harmony between what we are externally experiencing and what we are internally living.

This is what happened in Cathy's relationship to Chris. On the surface, he was a loving man who seemed to do and say all the right things. Yet, there was something that never felt right. Cathy believed it was just leftover emotions from her relationship to Bill, but intuitively, she could sense that Chris was not who he said he was. All her life, Cathy's Adaptable Self had not only survived but *thrived* in this dissonance.

Since she lived in the dis-regulated system of that Adaptable Self, she was not able to connect to the intuitive understanding that lived within. She had to first begin to develop relationships based on an emotionally regulated template, and she began that process with me. This is why the therapist must be working from a well-resourced, embodied place. Even if a client has their own dissonance, they are still able to sense if I am working from a dissonant place. Because if I am incongruent, it's going to be felt by them in that inter-subjective space between us. They have been thinking in that left-brain way all their life, accepting and adapting to others behaviors because, somatically, they have been so disconnected from their right hemisphere, they are not able to attend and attune to what their body is saying. Repair begins with co-regulation of the intersubjective field between therapist and client, and, ultimately, through the somatic empathy between people, where we are able to find and honor congruency between the left-brain story and the right-brain experience.

Since so many people come into therapy with attachment disorders, it is key that they are able to develop trust and feel secure in their ability to attach with a therapist. Because of this, many times, a client's unresolved issues will get projected upon the therapist. This transference is simply a fact. We are exploring developmental and shock trauma while engaging in a right-brain sensory experience. In order to develop a secure therapeutic relationship, the therapist needs to be first attuned to his or her own bodily-felt sensations. By self-regulating their own system, they will be better able to perceive the subtle cues of their clients, recognizing the shifts, rhythms, and internal dynamics of the other. In staying attuned to the shifting states of their client, the therapist is able to continually encourage their client to stay socially engaged and seek emotional regulation.

This somatic work attunes us into the present moment. It demands that we BE HERE NOW. By holding a place for left hemisphere thoughts, interpretations and internal self-talk, by observing subtle cues such as sensations, movements, and gestures, we begin to create the bridge from a left-brain narrative into a re-negotiated, embodied experience.

"I can hear Mom cooking in the kitchen overhead"

According to Tian Dayton, "Reenactment dynamics sounds a silent bell informing us as to where the pain lies." Experiential therapies were born out of psychodrama, a centuries-old form of therapy in which people would recall their life experiences to begin to reconnect with their emotional selves. Back in the 1930s, a psychologist by the name of Dr. Jacob Moreno first introduced group therapies to the American Psychiatric Association. Moreno believed in action therapy wherein the focus was less on traditional cognitive therapy promoted by doctors like Sigmund Freud and more on how our bodies use movement and gesture to express emotion. From his work, many more followed, using psychodrama and metaphor therapies to create a stage where "protagonists" could role-play and role reverse, beginning to express their stories through a right-brain experience. In the 1970s, Sharon Wegscheider-Cruse began to add music and art to these modalities as a way to amplify the experience.

Both Michelle and I were trained in this work, but as we continued in it over the years, we began to wonder whether we were helping people transform their trauma at the level that was most beneficial. There was no doubt that the experiential work was an important piece to re-negotiating painful life events, but as we learned more about somatic therapies, we began to see how the effects could also be implicitly repaired in the body. Because experiential was all about amplifying emotions, it often took people out of their Optimal Arousal Zones. We wanted to make sure the experiential therapies were rooted in a deep trust and social engagement. We found that when clients were in their Optimal Arousal Zone, they were better able to engage at a deeper level of therapeutic reparation.

By combining the somatic work and experiential therapies, we are able to oscillate between the left-brain understanding, and the right brain experience. Through such tools, we are able to bring implicit memory into conscious awareness. As the originator of psychodrama J.L. Moreno declared, "the psyche is an open system, constantly shaped—or misshaped—by the interactional environment in which human beings develop." This requires action and interaction, but just as importantly, Moreno believed, it demands spontaneity and creativity.

Through gesture, movement, sensation, and affect, people tell as much, if not more, of their story as they do through verbal language. It is not merely instinct that drives us but a series of fixed action patterns we have developed to adapt to our environment.

It is through somatic trust that we develop a deeper awareness of these indicators. The therapeutic relationship begins to concretize this underlying system of automatic action and understanding. In Cathy's case, we used SomEx^SM to highlight how she had learned to freeze in response to trauma, bringing that fixed action pattern into her relationships and Adaptable Self. She was then able to see the difference between appropriate response and her fixed action patterns of shutting down, which often only made her more vulnerable to trauma.

Cathy once told me a story about a particularly severe beating she and her sisters had experienced at the hands of their father:

> *Dad has told Ashley, Susan and me to sweep and mop the basement floor. It is a big floor. We take turns sweeping. It seems pretty clean. There is only dust and dirt. Someone says that if we just mop, it will get all the dust too, won't it? We decide to mop. Dad comes down to check on our progress. We are so proud that we are almost through. Suddenly, we are in trouble. We did not sweep. Dad beats us, and we have stay in our room for the rest of the day. We lie in our bed and cry together for a long time. I fall asleep. It is dinnertime when I wake up. Susan and Ashley are still asleep. I can hear Mom cooking in the kitchen overhead. I wonder if we will get to eat. I fall asleep and when I wake up, it is dark. The light in the laundry area is on, and Mom is putting clothes in the dryer. I ask her if I can eat. She says to go back to bed.*

Later, we brought that story into group, allowing Cathy to describe that moment in bed after the abuse. We began by focusing on the resources she utilized to deal with the pain. We also brought attention to resources presently available such as the group members and the safe space where so much healing had taken place. I then asked her to pick someone to play her father, and she chose one of the other members of the group, Tyrell. Then I asked for her to have someone re-create her mother's role, and she chose her group mate, Sharon. I suggested that Cathy move Tyrell and Sharon to where they stood in relationship to her in her childhood. She had Tyrell stand directly behind her and Sharon stand in front of her, with her back to Cathy. As Cathy stood sandwiched between them, facing no one herself, she began to cry.

"Cathy," I reminded her. "Can we take a moment and pay attention to your breathing?"

She slowed down, her breathing once again becoming grounded and rhythmic.

"How do you experience yourself standing between them?" I gently asked.

I could see her struggle to stay present and observe the early signs of dissociating. We paused here to orient and ground her before we continued in the process.

"Notice what's it's like to be here," I guided her. "I want you to tell me what this feels like."

"I can't," she stuttered.

"Cathy, what would help you stay present right now? Can you sense me next to you? Can you hear the music playing?"

She nodded her head. "It's just, it's not fair. She's just a little girl."

I asked for Cathy to pick someone to play herself as a child. She chose another group member, Leslie, to play her inner child who switched places with Cathy. Cathy's "inner child" now stood between her parents.

"How does that make you feel to see her there?" I asked Cathy.

"I don't know," she cried.

I brought out a chair and had her sit in it. I had noticed that Cathy's energy came out through her legs, and so I had her begin to move her feet against the ground, oscillating them to bring a rhythmic motion.

I kneeled in front of her and explained, "I think this is one of the stuck places where the feelings get coupled into a freeze state, Cathy. This is a place where the feelings are overwhelming and your system shuts down. In this dissociated state, your coping mechanisms begin to follow what was modeled in your mother's coping of an abusive marriage. You turn your back on that trauma, yet you are following in her footsteps."

I had noticed that Cathy seemed to have repressed energy in her legs as she shifted her weight between them. I had her begin to move her feet and legs against a large pillow prop, as we used movement to allow for the expression and release of the energy trapped inside.

"There you go," I whispered.

She began to cry. "I just don't know what else I'm supposed to do."

"I know," I replied, "but I bet that inside that little girl's actually a little ticked off."

Cathy's inner child still stood between her "parents," but now she began to call to Cathy, "Please, fight for me, I'm scared."

Cathy began to cry louder, asking me, "How do you fight against that?"

"I don't know, Cathy. But I bet you do."

She began to move her legs, pushing them into the pillow, and then she found her voice.

"No," she began to shout, her voice wavering with the word.

"It's okay to yell, Cathy. You can let it go."

As Cathy expressed her held emotions, moving from that frozen place where she had no control or choice, she became connected to her feelings and her voice. Cathy began to yell in a bold, primal tone of someone who was fully embodied yet well-resourced in the moment.

Finally, Cathy had discharged the repressed emotions, and I put on a song from her playlist, allowing her to connect with her child self and rest in that reparative moment as her group surrounded her, offering messages of support and love.

Cathy embraced Leslie as the two of them sat there holding one another. Cathy cried, thawing from the emotional freeze and experiencing the reawakening of those dissociated parts. Like the polar bear, her breathing began to calm, she had released the emotional toxins of those traumatic events while remaining grounded and oriented in the process.

As we went around the group afterwards giving feedback, Cathy confessed, "I realized my whole life, I keep submitting to people because I think that's what I need to survive. I had to submit my whole childhood, but that's just the adaptable part of me. My job now is to start protecting myself and that inner child inside."

Cathy had been submitting to her husbands for more years than she had been a child, spending over twenty five years begging and cajoling to try to gain back some of the power that had been taken from her when she was young. Finally she was learning what it was like to not submit, to begin to take her power back and take a stand for herself.

Moreno believed that whatever is learned in action must be unlearned in action. By staying in that action, Cathy was prevented from dissociating into her left hemisphere. She did not have to depend on her rationalizations and justifications—her defense mechanisms—but instead could express herself in a different way.

We are careful that through this work, we are not just increasing the state of activation, which can lead to more stress. This is why this work must be done in a safe and secure therapeutic environment. I was watching as Cathy did some releasing of emotion with her feet against the prop and noticed the expansion of her constricted Optimal Arousal Zone, creating space and tolerance for a more vibrant expression of her emotions. This is how gentle interventions of resources can help the client develop and strengthen resiliency.

"I saw how little there was of myself"

Resiliency is increased or enhanced through oscillating one's attention from the edge of what is painful to what is a resource. As Sharon Wegscheider-Cruse writes in *Choice Making*:

> Young children from [addict] homes become, in a sense, para-dependents… Just as the chameleon changes color to blend into its environment, para-dependent children alter external behavior for protective purposes. They can laugh, smile, and look surprised or serious in an instant. The exterior display—the public performance—completely hides the hurt, anger, shame, and loneliness within. A divided self results, a self that gets approval and acceptance for being an Adaptable Self, a secret self—the inner person no one knows.

For Cathy, she had perfected this divided self into adulthood. At church, on the soccer field, at PTA meetings, she was a well-organized and professional mother who managed to raise four children and still keep her marriage intact. But at night, she was the drug of someone else's addiction. Losing herself to her daytime identity, "mother and wife," she would dissociate from the victim role she played with Bill at night.

She would never be removed from her frozen state until she could begin to bridge those two identities by affirming the positive traits of herself that had always remained versus the adaptable qualities, which kept her sick. At one point in Cathy's treatment, she sent me a poem she had written to her first son:

> little stranger
> I longed to know you
> each time your little foot
> (or elbow,
> knee?)
> dashed against my ribs.
> Now suddenly
> we are two;
> already my voice quiets you
> across the vast expanse
> of cold white tile.
>
> You know me now
> inside and out;
> and even at this first
> best touching
> we are old friends.

If those words had been written by someone who had healthy attachments and strong boundaries, I would have said, "What a beautiful poem," but in my experience of Cathy, I wondered if it didn't also speak to how she learned to attach to others. She had never learned healthy boundaries, so how could she be expected to create them in the next generation? She was prepared for deep friendship, when really her role was to be an emotionally regulated caregiver.

According to Sharon Stanley, boundaries are the "energetic, spiritual, and emotional space that surrounds a person, helping [them] to have a sense of containment, self and safety from the environment. For most people who have grown up in a traumatic environment, they don't even know their boundaries are being violated because there are no boundaries in the household in the first place. Something can't be broken if it failed to exist in the first place.

In looking at Cathy's relationship, it was clear to see that until she could begin to have healthy boundaries with other adults, it was unlikely she would have them with her children.

By the time Cathy showed up on my doorstep, she had wrapped herself up so deeply in her children, she had ceased to exist. With each child, Cathy was able to focus more and more attention on someone else, and less on herself. When parents create these unhealthy attachments, they are trying to distract themselves from their own unmet needs.

Cathy had gotten to the place where she was unable to distinguish her own feelings, sensations, and thoughts from her family's. Their pains were her pains; their victories, her victories. Just as she had been unduly enmeshed with Bill, so she was with all four of her children—quite a vortex in which to lose one's self.

We eventually did a sculpt where I tried to show Cathy this entangled boundary violation. We had to have all the clients in the group participate in the sculpt to create the picture of her marriage and her children. In the sculpt, the group members "playing" Cathy's children all gathered around her. One by one, they all began to lean into Cathy.

"What's going on with you?" I asked Cathy.

She cleared her throat. "I can't breathe."

"Can you slow down a little a take in a breath of air?" I asked.

She did and nodded that she felt better.

Then I reminded her of a story she had told me about her childhood. That her mother had once said that as a baby she would stop breathing and that her mother would need to shake her to get her to start breathing again.

"When we stop breathing," I explained. "We start dying."

She nodded her head at me. Then I looked to the group, and asked, "I am wondering if any of you have ever been in a relationship where you felt you couldn't breathe. I am wondering what that might feel like to be with someone and love them so much that we can't even breathe."

I asked Cathy to consider the same question as she looked down at the ground.

"What's going on with you now, Cathy?"

"I'm looking at my feet but I don't feel connected to my body right now."

I went and stood down next to her as I asked, "I wonder how many times you have had to disappear because you couldn't handle the needs and affection of those around you? I wonder how many times you have lost yourself to your kids, your husband, your family. Probably a lot of times, lady."

Cathy smiled sadly as I told her, "It just occurred to me that I might be the first person you have ever had clear boundaries with."

"Yeah," she whispered.

"It might be about time to start creating some space where you can expand that skill."

I asked if using music would help resource the moment, putting on the playlist of songs Cathy had given me. We let the music fill up the room for a while as we noticed the effects somatically.

Cathy didn't move.

"Cathy," I called to her, "would you be willing to stand with me?"

At first her movement was slow, but as she raised her head up and made eye contact with me, she began to get centered and grounded in the moment.

I asked her what this sculpt should look like in order to give her the space that was appropriate for her. She moved her group members into a circle with each other, and then she stood on the outside.

She smiled at me, "That way I can protect them."

"Yes, that's good. But what else can you do?"

"I can move around too."

When working with boundary issues, sometimes having the client look from both perspectives, looking from both inside and outside the picture, he or she can create a healthier interpretation of the circumstance. By moving Cathy in and out of the sculpt, she was able to get more comfortable with being free of enmeshing with her children. She was having the opportunity to be more choiceful about what she was experiencing (salience) and her value judgment of it (valence). Initially, the boundary violation was the place of comfort, but as she saw the perspective from both vantage points, she could claim her need for healthier boundaries. She began to feel empowered.

"I just saw a falling star"

From the first day Cathy came to me, she had trouble accepting that Chris, her so-called "knight in shining armor," was a sex addict, just like Bill. She knew something wasn't right, and certainly the affair helped her to put it into words, but she thought the perpetrator behavior was part of being married. She had been groomed since childhood to believe perpetration and betrayal were synonymous with love.

Just as in the boundary work, we had to begin to connect her with reality—to integrate those rationalizations and minimizations of the left brain with the effects of trauma that get stored in the body. For most of psychotherapy's history, the idea was always that cognitive behavioral therapies should utilize a left-hemisphere, top-down approach. These modalities believed that through traditional talk therapy, the symptoms of trauma would be managed and the typical defenses deconstructed. That's not to say that this process doesn't play a role. Sitting across from me in my office, Cathy participated in various modalities, including cognitive behavioral work, but doing cognitive work alone would have kept those sensations trapped in somatizations.

The left hemisphere processes data from a top-down perspective, which is necessary for understanding our environment. The left hemisphere experiences the intake of information before communicating it to the rest of the body. It is through the right hemisphere's use of neuroception that we take in information via a bottom-up processing. Afferent information moves sensory experiences inward, through the neurons that go up the spine and into the brainstem and the cortex. This process consists of 80% of the information we receive. Efferent information is transmitted through neurons that go down from the cortex into the body, and make up for 20% of the information received. Therefore, this bottom up processing is nearly ten times faster, and is what we use when we're sensing our environment and in particular, danger.

This also speaks to why a somatic based approach to therapy is much more powerful than a cognitive-based approach, because so much of our life story is held in the body, allowing for a more comprehensive integration for the client. It is through the ability of the process known as neuroception that we are able to sense and experience our environment. Our bodies are able to gather information and then send the signals to the brain. This is the same process by which babies are able to sense a stranger or communicate distress based on their own neuroception.

We need to integrate and work both bottom-up and top-down, which is why therapy is most effective when using both approaches, allowing for a more comprehensive experience for the client. As noted psychiatrist Dr. Alan Schore explains, we must create "an interactive process of communication that helps to process emotions (conscious and unconscious) through new and ongoing, affectively charged relational or regulatory experiences."

Cathy had learned in childhood that to process emotion was to invite further trauma. She and her siblings were not allowed to cry after their beatings. Often they were sent to bed or sent off to play afterwards. In Cathy's relationship with with Bill, she learned that to fight back or reject Bill's advances only made him all the more aggressive. It was easier to "just take it," as she explained to me.

And she did. For over twenty years. When Cathy first started telling the story of Bill's sexual addiction to the group, I had to keep reminding them and her that these events were not once or twice over the course of a marriage, but every day over many years. The sexual behaviors that were present in her relationship with Bill were not congruent with Cathy's value system. Instead, she adapted herself to meet Bill's needs, thus re-enacting her childhood trauma.

Cathy had long lost her ability to protect herself from violence. In fact, her defensive systems were greatly impaired by years of chronic stress. As psychologist Dave Berger explains, "Proper functioning of the sensory systems (visual, auditory, proprioceptive, etc.) is another critical element in the overall mechanism of self-protection. As with motor reflexes, sensory systems may be disrupted due to trauma. In order for the threat response cycle to function properly, the sensory systems and motor functions that contribute to the ability to orient and defend must be integrated, functional, and available."

Cathy could do neither when she first started in therapy. Due to the sustained traumas she experienced, Cathy would often freeze and become unable to respond when injury presented itself. The pattern of brace, collapse, and rebound became a lifestyle. Bill would make his advances, she would brace herself for their success, then collapse after his assault, before rebounding back into the mother/wife role she wore like a badge of honor. This Adaptable Self thrives in rebound, getting energized by the hyper aroused state and moving the person back to their familiar roles.

I asked Cathy to recall a time when she was a child where all had felt right with the world, where she felt connected and present. She told me the story of seeing her first shooting star:

> *Five houses face each other, sharing a huge lawn. The Williamsons live at the top of the hill. The Williamson kids are camping out on the big lawn. We have two big bedspreads spread out on the ground, and we each have our own blanket and pillow. The sky is purple dark and the stars are very bright. Everyone else is asleep. I feel warm and safe. I feel like I did in church when we were singing I Stand All Amazed. A star falls from the sky. I wake Ashley up. I just saw a falling star. We lie there and watch, with our heads together, and two more stars fall. I fall asleep watching, with my face next to Ashley's.*

Cathy had been in group for six months at that point. She knew the other members well, and had established a strong bond of trust with them, and with me. I asked that Cathy close her eyes as she described the night of the falling star. One of the other members played her sister Ashley, who sat close to her.

What I try to do is use the voices, the scripts and memories from the family system to connect people both into their healthy attachments as well as the resourced experiences where they have found healing. As "Ashley" began to ask Cathy about the beautiful starry night, I asked Cathy if there were messages from her family that blocked her from enjoying these positive experiences in life.

"Aren't the stars beautiful tonight, Sissy?" the group member roleplaying Ashley asked. "It's so peaceful up there."

As "Ashley" offered gentle messages from a childhood summer night, Cathy shared the other messages she heard as a child, things that her parents had said to her, such as calling her too sensitive. She went on to recall that later in life Bill would offer similar messages, telling her she was too sensitive and defective because of what happened to her in childhood.

I replied, "As you tell us about those messages, what do you notice about Ashley sitting next to you now?"

Cathy realized she had disconnected from the feelings of joy and innocence she was having with her sister under the stars. I invited her to consider this as a dynamic that had played itself out in her life, where joy and innocence would often be hijacked by shame.

Building on that Somatic Trust that Cathy had with the group and me, we were able to honor Cathy's efforts, supporting her as she claimed her strength and the power to speak her truth.

I asked her to pay attention to this experience with Ashley, to stay focused on her messages as we began to uncouple feelings of joy from those sensations of shame. This became a lifelong re-enactment for Cathy in that she deprived herself of having joy because it would be attached to deep feelings of shame and low self-worth.

At this point, we utilized the group members to offer affirming messages to Cathy that allowed for the amplification of her loving attachment to her sister. From that place she was asked to identify her own affirmations to counter the messages given by others, and with a smile, she offered, "I love my sister, and I appreciate my sensitivity."

As implicit memory and right hemisphere integrate, life force, vitality, and energy return. Resiliency is increased, and new meaning emerges. Again, most of this work should not be performed alone. Like all relationships, it takes more than one person to create a community, and in order to heal trauma and shame, we need to heal in community.

Before continuing in this book, look for those you can turn to for empathy in your life. We all have the ability to create a family of choice—those three to five people who are able to care and support us in our recovery process. They represent a safe family system, but just as importantly, they help us to begin developing somatic trust between people who are also trying to repair and recover their own wounds. This trust can begin with a therapist, but it can also be amplified and enhanced by developing a family of choice.

If you are lacking these companions, where can you begin to find some? Are there twelve-step meetings in your area? Are there other support services or spiritual groups that are available? Can you search for a therapist who is versed in this work? Are there group therapies are available to you?

Review what kind of self-care and attunement you could begin practicing to create more awareness and authenticity in your own life.

1. How do you nurture yourself today – through massage or bodywork, through exercise or hobbies? How do you reward yourself by allowing that Authentic Self to prevail?

2. How do you still fail to nurture yourself? Where do you still deny yourself happiness or what behaviors do you participate in that either limit or shame that Authentic Self?

3. How could you begin to include others in this process? Who would you like with you as you try new hobbies or new experiences? Who would be a part of your new family of choice?

It is hard to trust others when we have lost ourselves to the relationships around us but through re-negotiating our own life stories, by rebuilding our sense of value and worth, we begin to find and attract communities in which trust thrives, and in which we can begin to heal.

BRAIN BASICS BY MICHELLE
OPTIMAL AROUSAL ZONE

The Optimal Arousal Zone is the regulated space between sympathetic activated arousal and parasympathetic collapse. In this space, we are able to live in well-regulated emotional harmony. Harmony is a vibrant, active place. The goal is not about living flat-lined, on only one plane of emotional experience, but, rather, restoring vitality to the system and allowing for oscillations between the edges of the parasympathetic and sympathetic states. Often people will think that the absence of emotional activation is healthy, that we are never supposed to be mad or sad, but vitality and harmony live within all emotions and feelings. It is about experiencing and integrating joy and sadness, anger and peace in a way that can be felt in an embodied way. When people are in high activation, it is as though the emotional faucet is broken and flooding the system; when they are in collapse, it is completely turned off. Regulation is about restoring that emotional output to a natural, resourceful stream.

The levels of the Optimal Arousal Zone are as follows:

Emotional Arousal Scale

15	Out of Control	Too Intense
14	Overwhelmed	Too Fast
13	Losing My Grip	Too Much
12	Not Grounded	
11	Feeling Light	
10		
9		
8	Safe and Happy	
7		
6		
5	Feeling Heavy	
4	Sad	No Energy
3	Depressed	Too Tired
2	Hopeless	Too Scary
1	Despair	Shut Down

Based on Somatic Transformation Optimal Arousal Zone. © S. Hobson 2011

When someone is highly activated, the goal is to ground and stabilize them so that they can begin to experience life in a regulated state. For those who are frozen, it is about restoring them to vitality. If they are in the Optimal Arousal Zone, they are in a ventral vagal state, but that place can only be achieved through resourcing, grounding, and orienting techniques that allow the person to move out of that frozen or hypo aroused state.

109

The movement is facilitated by a safe therapeutic alliance between client and therapist. Once a client has trust in the process, they can begin to oscillate within the Optimal Arousal Zone—finding tolerance and flexibility—and begin attuning to the shifts and changes that occur while skirting its edges. This window of tolerance between the parasympathetic and sympathetic states grows over time, allowing for better emotional regulation even in traumatic or emotionally-charged environments.

Just because we are trying to live a more emotionally regulated life doesn't mean life will stop moving. This isn't about turning that faucet off. It is about learning how to live in an emotionally abundant way that doesn't flood us.

CHAPTER FIVE

Somatic Modification

There is always a point in the therapeutic effort when, after months of therapy and some substantial progress, one of my clients will want to stop everything and run. It's understandable. And I've been guilty of it too. I'll admit, my first therapy experience was not the one that changed my life. Far from it. When I finally got into enough pain, I realized I needed to start doing a deeper level of therapeutic work before I wound up drunk...or dead.

It all happened when I was two years sober. I had decided to quit smoking. Though I expected to feel relieved from the addiction—I had been smoking since I was a teenager—I instead felt weighted down with an incredible anxiety, getting so physically ill from the tension that I ended up being hospitalized for stomach problems.

After months of this, the doctors decided there was more going on than just nicotine withdrawal. Though I had managed to put down the alcohol and drugs with far less severe physical consequences, I had been holding on to my last vestige of addiction, using nicotine to keep my emotions contained. But once the cigarettes were gone, forget it, there was nothing left to separate me from the fear and pain lying beneath.

It was recommended that I go see a therapist and that was when I was first introduced to experiential therapy. Though I didn't know the words at the time, my therapist was able to communicate with me in ways that few others could. She was in recovery herself and from that first meeting, I could feel a connection with her. Though I didn't understand the science behind her behavior, I would come to learn that my therapist was helping to build an intersubjective field between us, in which she could attune to me emotionally and, in turn, help me become aware of feelings myself. This was a place of deep empathy—not one filled with the distant, clinical exchange I had felt so many other times in therapy. She offered me compassion and reverence, honoring the wounded addict sitting before her. Though there were times when I wanted to quit, when I wanted to say, "Screw this," and walk out, she kept challenging me to look in the mirror, to find the person hiding behind the anger and fear and stomach pains that had taken over my life.

Which is why when I am sitting across from a client and I feel that inflexibility in them rise up, I try to hold up the same loving mirror—not the one that shows them all their flaws, but the one that tries to show them the truth behind the veil, knowing that healing will only happen if they stick around for the work.

Often the moment we are in our greatest resistance is the moment we are closest to transformation. It is the dark night of the soul, where we have slammed ourselves up against that last impenetrable wall, and are finally willing to surrender. For so many of my clients and myself, we failed to see the door because we were too busy hitting our heads against the wall. As they say, that which you resist, persists.

For Cathy, she had similarly spent her whole life attempting to get help only to rebuff the aid when it arrived. Searching for the solution and being willing to accept it are two very different things. Cathy would read self-help books in isolation. She would find therapists but only stick around for a few sessions. She would reach out to people but then always pull back, trapped in a terrible purgatory of her own addictions and codependency. Finally, she had enough and became willing to try something new.

Somatic work does not take place over night. It is a committed effort to recovery and repair in which the client participates in various forms of therapy, such as individual and group sessions. Once trust and connection are created, the client and therapist work towards utilizing more tools, bringing awareness to those parts formerly dissociated or compartmentalized. The process allows them to try to stretch the Optimal Arousal Zone to tolerate feelings or memories that were previously unbearable. By incorporating resources to strengthen the vagal tone, we can work to touch the edges of the hyper or hypo areas to integrate lost or frozen parts. Though Cathy resisted much of the initial work, slowly, she began to see the effectiveness of the process—her transformation had begun.

"If I could fix myself everything would be okay"

As Judith and Allan Schore explain in their piece "Modern Attachment Theory" for the *Clinical Social Work Journal,* "Attachment theory is deceptively simple on the surface: it posits that the real relationships of the earliest stage of life indelibly shape us in basic ways and that for the rest of the life span, attachment processes lie at the center of human development."

When Cathy was ten, she told her mother that her eyes wanted to stay closed all the time. She knew this was a problem, that this was not how life was supposed to be processed, but, at ten years old, she lacked the language or comprehension to see it for what it was. Her mother told her everyone felt that way, which only further normalized the behavior. From that point forward, Cathy didn't see her desire to sleep as a form of escape, she saw it as part of life, believing that everyone felt that way. By the time Cathy reached high school, reading books on psychology had become common for her, either through textbooks or the traditional self-help library of M. Scott Peck and others. There is a reason this field is crowded with experts and stories, psychologists and theories, because people have been aching for a solution for generations. Read at night when the children go to bed, kept on the nightstand in easy reach, so many people hope that if they could just find the right book, follow the right steps in the quiet of their home, they will be okay. After years of trying this method, Cathy found herself frustrated and seeking more.

When she got married, Cathy began a long battle to find therapy through the church, and though she initially found support through the local ministry, Bill ultimately intervened:

> *Whenever I mentioned counseling to Bill (which was not often), he would launch into a soap box about therapy not doing anyone any good except the therapist, who got rich from it. Later, I reached out to the Church, and tried to talk with a minister about my problems. I thought that if I only there were a way for me to behave as a better Christian wife, Bill would behave more like a better Christian husband. But when one of the ministers asked that I not be so candid about my relationship, my shame only got worse. I already felt so wrong, and now I was being told even from my faith that I was wrong. Finally, through a friend, I found a therapist who would see me on a sliding scale. But when Bill found out he threw an absolute fit and said that I had gone behind his back and demeaned his position as leader at home.*

Over the years Cathy had submitted to Bill's sexual advances, acquiesced to Chris's affair, and by the end, had become completely enmeshed with her children. Something in her finally said, "Something's got to change." And though at the start, her quest for counseling came out of a codependent call, she ended up staying for herself.

Once we began our work, Cathy and I developed a therapeutic relationship based in safety and empathy. In Marjorie Rand and Babette Rothschild's article on "Somatic Empathy" by the same title, they define the practice as, "The capacity and action of understanding, being aware of, being sensitive to and vicariously experiencing in one's body, the sensations, thoughts, feelings and experiences of another (either past or present), without having the feelings, sensations, thoughts and experiences fully communicated in an objective, explicit manner."

As Cathy's story began to unfold, I could feel and watch her move outside her Optimal Arousal Zone, noticing which stories pushed her into sympathetic arousal and which sent her into a dorsal vagal collapse. Much like my own first experiential therapist, I could help create an inter-subjective field between us, which allowed me to track her gestures and expressions through my own sensory awareness. I would watch how her feet moved, how her eyes focused on one object or failed to focus on anything, and I could pick up, through my own right brain home of sensory awareness, how her stories were pushing her above or below her arousal zone. Through this process, I was able to offer empathy and support, but I was also able to create boundaries around her responses to keep her from moving too far outside her Optimal Arousal Zone.

For me, it is about honoring a client's choices as they discover their path. The dialogue between client and therapist should be invitational, it should be held with safety and deep reverence for the experience of the client and the magnificent ways in which the body and mind copes with trauma. And though I don't believe in preaching religion or forcing spirituality on any of my clients, I do believe in tapping into that Divine spirit that I often see peeking out behind the person sitting on my office couch. I recognize that in creating that neurological connection, we are mimicking a spiritual one, communicating not through words or action but through that magical right-brain understanding and compassion of which we are all capable. As Allan Schore explains, "In monitoring counter-transferential responses, the clinicians' right brain tracks at a preconscious level not only the arousal rhythms and flows of the patient's affective states, but also her own interceptive bodily-based affective responses to the patient's implicit facial, gestural, and prosodic communications."

It is why so many of us seek the spiritual experience—because we want to see our life story mirrored in a way that is Divine, in a way that it is understood wholly and with benevolence. It is lifting up that veil and showing the client the Truth that lies beyond.

By bypassing the heavily defended left-brain, we are able to invite dialogue from the right hemisphere. Instead of consistently strengthening the defenses of the left, you begin to strengthen the body-based communication of the right. This is why the body-based therapies, such as breath work, Reiki, movement, art, etc., are so powerful. They teach attunement and resonance, allowing for the client to feel in their body where the sensory responses are taking place. They begin to develop tracking skills, understanding where certain stimuli are affecting their sensory systems. Through this process of inquiry and modification, the client begins to integrate that left-brain understanding of the experience with the right brain's responses to it. Through such work, therapist and client develop an "earned attachment." Both are entering into a well ordered, regulated, and resourced relationship with clear boundaries and containment. It is in this space that we can attend to the "unending intricacies embedded in awareness" as described by Don Johnson and Ian Grand in *The Body in Psychotherapy*. By watching how the breath moves, how the body responds, the therapist can help create the intersubjective field I found in that first therapeutic effort, the one that finally made me say, "Something's got to change."

The body has an innate natural rhythm, that song of the Divine Self, but is unable to attend to it when in a state of flight, fight or freeze. This is why we have to work within the felt sense, bringing awareness and modification to the somatic cues that take place between client and therapist. As the Schores write, these "nonverbal affective and thereby mind/body communications are expressions of the right brain, which is centrally involved in the analysis of direct kinesthetic information received by subject from his own body, an essential implicit process."

After forty years of looking for someone to explain to her why she wanted to close her eyes all the time, Cathy's eyes began to open. She began to grow in her awareness and attachment to the therapeutic effort.

And then she decided she wanted to throw it all away.

"I didn't trust you at all"

A number of years back, Michelle and I realized that sometimes group and individual sessions were not enough. We wanted to create an intensive retreat where people could immerse themselves in the process, removing themselves from the distractions and invasions of their daily lives. By pulling them out of their patterns, they were able to create more awareness around their behaviors. Instead of worrying about fulfilling their daily tasks, they could begin to focus entirely on themselves. They could begin to share and express that life story with a therapeutic community who also desired change for themselves.

In order to make meaning out of life, the left-brain narrative posits that we are terminally unique. Our defense mechanisms translate this narrative into a story that further alienates us from our fellows. This is particularly true when the left brain is trying to compartmentalize and minimize twenty years of sexual abuse. Cathy needed to re-connect with a world in which her story was not an isolated, insular event. It was important for her to share her story with others and to recognize she didn't hold the patent on pain and betrayal.

Two days before that first trauma retreat, Cathy called me and said that she wasn't going. I listened as she explained that she had too much to do, that her family couldn't make it without her for the week.

"Cathy," I asked, "how long have you been married?"

"To Chris or to Bill?" she asked.

"To both. Actually, since you were only divorced from Bill for a year before marrying Chris, why don't we just consider them one big long marriage. How long since you first married Bill?"

"Well…" I could hear her voice tense over the phone.

"Cathy, I am just wondering how long you have committed yourself to both of those relationships."

"It would have been twenty-nine years in January."

"Okay, good," I replied. "Now, if you're children survived you being in those marriages for twenty-nine years, I am sure they will survive six days of you participating in an intensive."

Cathy promptly hung up on me, but I am used to that. Most therapists should be. Thirty minutes later she called back and said, "I'll see you on Friday."

Prior to the retreat, Cathy had given me another story about her molestation, one in which she explained how the trauma had been repeated over and over. Cathy discovered that she wasn't the only victim in her family. Two of her other sisters were also molested by the local man, but her older sister, Patty, told their mother about it, putting an end to their visits. In the story, she described what happened:

> *We are in the kitchen at Mr. Jackson's house. His wife is not there. Patty is on his lap. Suddenly it is time to go home. When we get home, Patty goes into the bedroom*

with Mom and Dad. When they come out, Mom tells us not to go over to Mr. Jackson's house any more.

Several days later, I am walking down the road and Mr. Jackson drives by. He stops and backs up. He says, "Did your parents tell you not to come to my house anymore?" I act like I can't understand what he says. He repeats it. I again act like I can't hear him. He says, "Come closer." I step closer to the car and he asks again, "Did your parents tell you not to come to my house anymore?" I say yes. His face changes and it makes my stomach go cold. Then he looks at me, kind of sad, and says, "Okay. That's probably best." He drives away.

I am scared and confused. When I get home I tell my mom that Mr. Jackson stopped his car and asked me if my parents told me not to go to his house any more. She turns around to face me and asks sharply, "What did you say to him?" I tell her I acted like I didn't hear him.

Cathy had told me how when she was a child, they had a pet beagle named Charlie. She would lie in a grassy section of her backyard with Charlie, a little area hidden from view of her house, and she would tell him all her secrets. She would sit next to Charlie with one hand in his fur, the other grabbing at the green moss, picking pieces out as she stared up at the sky, and there, Cathy would find a little space to be herself. I found some green felt material that Cathy could as a resource and a reminder of her time in the backyard. The brain has an ability to respond the same way to a stimulus, whether the sensation is real or imagined, which is why props are so effective in our work.

I asked Cathy if there was anyone who could play Charlie. She chose her friend, Ryan, with whom she shared the story of having a violent father. I asked that Cathy sit down on the material and that Ryan sit beside her and hold her hand.

"Cathy, I just want to ask you to use some visualization here, and to feel the soft moss below you."

Cathy's left hand began to rub the "grass," moving slowly as I asked, "Can you tell me what that feels like? Feel that sensation against your fingertips, the palm of your hand? Can you notice how your body experiences the touch and how it felt to lay on the moss?"

She replied, "Well it was kind of soft, and I remember it being so quiet. It was my own secret spot."

I sat down beside her. "What was it like in your family to have something that was yours?"

"I didn't have anything that was mine. Except Charlie."

"No you didn't," I replied. "Why don't you go ahead and connect with Charlie and tell me how that feels."

Tears filled her eyes as Cathy and Ryan held hands, "It feels good. It feels safe."

"So just be here in this secret safe place. You might want to take a moment and let the felt sense of the experience imprint in your imagery, keeping this moment in your heart. This was yours and no one could touch you here. Take your time with that."

Cathy's eyes filled with more tears. "Just breathe," I reminded her. "This was your escape, where you had someone you could trust and a safe space where no one could find you."

Cathy began to tell me, "I would pull off the roses from a nearby bush and take the ones that hadn't opened and try to push the buds through."

She suddenly began to cry harder. Then she laughed, "I didn't think talking about the roses would make me cry."

I mirrored back what she had just told to me. "I didn't think talking about the roses would make me cry."

I let Cathy stay in her resourced place for a few more moments and then I asked Cathy if she was willing to address the unresolved issues around the abuse. I could see her body tense, her hand pausing for a moment from rubbing the grass.

"Okay, Cathy. Let's slow down and notice what you're experiencing. Feel how your breath has changed, find your center again, that calm awareness you had with Charlie."

Cathy asked Ray, another one of her group members to play "Mr. Jackson."

I handed Ray a rope, and then I had Cathy ask someone else to play "Fantasy."

She chose Tammy, a newer, younger member of the group, who got up and took hold of the other end of the string. I then asked Cathy to grab the middle part of the string with her left hand, still holding onto to Ryan with her right. I directed Ray and Tammy to begin to pull on opposite sides of the string, as Cathy was slowly moved from side to side in between them.

"Do you feel that movement, Cathy?"

She nodded.

"And where do you feel that?"

She didn't respond at first so I reminded her to center herself, connect with her breathing. As she inhaled, she nodded. "It's in my stomach."

I watched as she kept swaying between the two role players, letting them rock her.

"Damn, you're just pulled between the abuse and the fantasy, aren't you?"

Cathy smiled sadly. And then as she started to cry, I knelt down and began to speak quietly to her. "Thank God you had that fantasy, but then that fantasy got caught up in the abuse, didn't it?"

Cathy nodded, lightly holding onto the string. I asked her, "Where in the body are you noticing anything in this moment?"

Cathy looked around the room for an answer. "I feel it in my chest."

"Notice what the sensation is like?"

"I just want to run," she explained.

"I hear you," I replied. "How can we utilize this space to honor the held energy in your legs?"

"I don't know," Cathy replied, her face beginning to strain.

"Let's breathe, Cathy. Find your breath. Maybe begin pushing through your legs."

Suddenly Cathy laughed. "I just feel like my heart is going to jump out. I can't stay still, but I can't escape. It's like I have nowhere to go, but I don't want to stay where I am. It's what I would sometimes feel with Bill. Just this desire to run."

"Are you willing to connect with someone in group either with eyes or touch?" Referring to her group member Ryan who was standing in for Charlie, I asked. "Can you look at Charlie and notice what comes up for you when you recall him as a resource?"

"It feels safe; he's mine and no one else's."

I stood up and ask the group members playing "Fantasy" and "Mr. Jackson" to begin tugging the string harder.

"Okay, stay with Charlie, Cathy, but see what happens when these opposing forces start pulling you? What happens when you are pulled between trauma and escape?"

Cathy began to breathe faster as she sat there, the rope pulling her back and forth.

I directed her to pay attention to her breath, grounding and centering her as Fantasy and Mr. Jackson tried to pull her back and forth.

"Try to stay with the experience, stay connected to your resources, Cathy."

I watched as Cathy's breathing became shallower, her muscles constricted, and her body bracing itself, much like watching a skittish horse preparing to run from a predator. In many ways, we react to fear in the much same way a horse does. Our muscles tense. We want to run. Or, like a caged animal who knows neither how to escape nor to fight, we freeze in response to the terror.

At EHC, we offer equine therapy, so I have had the chance to watch how horses behave, how their nervous systems seem so deftly attuned to ours. Often, as I sit across from a client I will imagine them as one of those majestic yet restless creatures. Over many millions of years, horses evolved a unique and highly tuned nervous system that has been necessary for their survival in the wild. Like all animals, like us, they have evolved to respond to the environment around them in ways that protect them from predators.

Because horses lack baring teeth or claws to attack, they must rely on their autonomic nervous system's arousal abilities to protect them from the world. Using their sensory systems to communicate and defend, horses continuously receive information from the external environment (sight, sound, smell, taste, touch) and from within the body (position, temperature, pain) to determine the best way for them to respond to a threat. I could see Cathy's legs making a pushing motion when we were involved in the story. Her natural response to perpetration was to run, but at the time, this response was thwarted. Now, in this work, she was able to move her legs in an attempt to defend herself.

We placed a pillow again in front of her and allowed her to keep moving while she developed what she needed to be able to say to her trauma and to her escape. She turned to her perpetrator and clearly said, "Don't touch me there."

Then, while still holding Ryan's hand, she turned to "Fantasy" and said, "Thank you for helping me survive. I don't need you anymore."

By integrating the sense-memory of that time with the left-brain narrative of the experience, her legs then relaxed. She let go of the rope.

If resiliency is the body's ability to tolerate stress and still bounce back to a place of integrated living, we need to start the inquiry with a well-regulated and comprehensive approach to what it means to be *in* one's body. The reason humans don't recover from trauma as well as animals, as in the story of the polar bear, is that we over-rely on our left brain's defense mechanisms and compartmentalize our body-based sensations. When a wild animal is caught by a predator, they are able to integrate and process the trauma through their deeply connected somatic instincts. Wild animals don't experience Post Traumatic Stress Disorder because they are able to release the body-held effects of the trauma. But for humans, the wild looks a little bit different. Our predators often live in our own homes. What do you do if your predator is your parent? How do you repair from trauma that happened years ago, when there was no way to protect or defend yourself? How can we ever bounce back? And how do we repair when we are still sharing a bed with the source of our trauma?

That was the work I was asking of Cathy, urging that she begin exploring her sense awareness. As noted psychologist Ernest Rossi writes in *The Psychobiology of Mind-body Healing*, "All the sensory-perceptual modalities are involved, vision and imagery, audition, proprioception-kinesthesia, smell, taste, and all possible combinations of these as they are expressed in significant aspects of mind-body communication and human identity."

Our clients begin to focus on the following elements of their sensory awareness, creating meditations around the work to better develop the right brain:

- Tactile – In exploring the interior of the skin, I ask that clients pretend they are using a mini-camera to explore the texture and sensation of skin. What do they notice as they experience the interior of their body? I might ask them to start at the top of their head and scan through their whole body, noticing where they are holding tension or experiencing relaxation.

- Auditory – Take a moment and notice the environment and be aware of what you take in through the ears. What do you hear and what can you tune out in terms of external noise? What happens when you try to pay attention to the world around you? Take a moment to listen to the world inside of you.

- Taste – What tastes are soothing and comforting? Notice how your mouth, tongue, and saliva respond to the memory or imagery of certain foods and flavors?
- Smell – Are there smells you are sensitive to? Are there scents that are particularly relaxing and comforting? Try some different essential oils and explore which ones are pleasant and notice what feelings they might bring up.

Though Cathy bucked initially at the idea of going to the intensive retreat, trying to escape before she even found out what it might be like to stay, afterwards, she called me.

"I noticed this morning that I wanted to run," she told me.

"And what did you do with that?"

"I began to pay attention, and then I allowed myself to remember the moss, to find that resourced place. Instead, I went outside for a walk. I paid attention to the cool air on my face, the slight breeze through my hair. I could smell hibiscus in the air. I felt alive. I felt good."

"I finally had a space to experience my feelings"

One of the reasons we ask folks to write out their life history is to bridge that deep disconnection between the left brain world of logic and language and the right brain home of sensory experience. As Cathy was to learn, telling her story about the abuse she suffered in her marriage to Bill was a long way off from negotiating it. As she wrote about their relationship:

> *It started as a power struggle over the shower. If I got into the shower first Bill would come in and have sex*

125

> *with me. I would tell him that I didn't want to have sex in the shower because it was my time—my time to think, to pray, to prepare for the day ahead. But he just ignored me and kept making me have sex whenever he caught me in there. Instead, I started letting him go to the shower first and then I would get in after he was gone for work. One morning though I had to get up before him and so I decided I would just lock the door. We had one of those skeleton key locks and the key had been missing for years. I thought that would definitely keep him out. I am in the shower and suddenly I hear him at the door. He can see its locked and then there is silence. Minutes later he comes back and is picking that damn thing. He must have gotten a screwdriver or something but the entire time I am in the shower, he is working to get that door open, and as soon as he did, he was on me.*

In trauma bonding, both parts of the autonomic nervous system are over stimulated and begin to couple together. Like Chinese fingercuffs, we get stuck between that hypo and hyper arousal, and the more we try to pull out of one, we get trapped in the other. Caught between acceleration and deceleration, our emotional system becomes jammed, unable to properly process and respond to stimuli. Bill's consistent and assaulting behavior led Cathy to live in this state, but it doesn't take such volatile behavior to trigger the same response.

SomEx^{SM} is based on an understanding of the body and nervous system, through which we can process past experiences without the heightened activation that may shut them down. We attempt to access the client's reaction to exploring their histories while guiding them to stay within the Optimal Arousal Zone. Recognizing that our biographies become our biology, we are able to bring attention to the held or frozen experiences that block us from the authentic integration of ourselves. Through techniques such as tracking sensation and oscillation, we are able to restore rhythm and regulation to the psyche. In doing so, clients like Cathy are able to integrate the story with the sensory experience of the present moment.

Cathy and I discussed presenting her sexual timeline to the group through the experiential work, but first we agreed to try an exercise where she would share the story of Bill's abuse in the shower to gauge her comfort level and her ability to stay within the Optimal Arousal Zone. In the next group session, I arranged an elastic band between Cathy and the rest of the group, which she could use as a visual representation of a boundary. When she began to feel uncomfortable in her story, she could focus her attention on the elastic boundary, expanding it or constricting it to reflect her comfort level. I wanted to give her a tangible buffer so that she could speak from a safe place, creating that subjective field that honored Cathy's need for privacy while asking her to exercise her trust in the group. She needed to spend some time being inside the boundary, imagining what that would feel like to actually have one, in order for her to safely reveal and maintain her vulnerability. As she shared later, "I finally began to have a space in which to experience my feelings."

Throughout the exercise, we worked to make sure that Cathy stayed grounded and centered. We would pause to orient her breathing and her awareness of the room and the group sitting on the other side of the boundary, helping her to notice when there was a tendency to get triggered. The goal of the piece was for Cathy to be able to talk about her abuse while still staying present. By slowing uncoupling the freeze states where the gas and the brakes are going at the same time, we were able create some repair around those stuck places. Similarly, Cathy was able to self-regulate without collapsing into a freeze state. Throughout the exercise, she kept her eyes open, not burying her face in her hands as she had often done before. Instead, she spoke with a calm strength, and in a state of conscious awareness. She was working within the safe space of the Optimal Arousal Zone where she could process and repair the trauma without coupling the sympathetic arousal and dorsal vagal collapse. In trauma, the sympathetic arousal and dorsal vagal parts of the nervous system are working concurrently. Repair is the attempt to ease the tension held in both systems. By releasing that held energy, the client is able to reorganize their experience in an integrated and regulated way. Instead of responding like that root-bound tree at Home Depot, toppling over from the slightest push, Cathy was finally starting to plant roots in her recovery.

By using the elastic band, Cathy was able to experience an increased sense of protectiveness and vulnerability. Props allow clients to make the work more vivid, activating their imagination and their implicit memory to recall an experience, yet at the same time staying grounded in the work to begin strengthening their ventral vagal tone. In many ways, the props provide a symbol that can be used to amplify the therapeutic process. When we have a client that is grounded in a resource, we may use props, music, or art to amplify.

As Cathy told me later, "I don't know that I would have ever made it to the level of the Reconstruction Day had I not taken those first steps of trusting the process. It was those first small changes in perception that led me to begin to make the big changes in behavior. None of that would have happened without strengthening my ability to process emotion."

Through somatic empathy, inquiry, interventions, and modifications, we can be restored to our Optimal Arousal Zones. There we can begin to re-negotiate the trauma, oscillating in small shifts between sympathetic arousal and safety, and between dorsal vagal freeze and safety. This dance is what brings us into harmony, allowing for trauma to be re-organized. As famed psychologist Tian Dayton explains in her book *A Living Stage*, "Scene-setting, through descriptive words or even props, can also function as a warm-up as the protagonist goes through the motions and narrates what he is doing. Grounding what has lived in the imagination can feel evocative and stimulate memories that need to be recognized and respected."

"Dad pulls me closer to him, and strokes my hair"

According to Jaak Panskepp's article, "The Core Emotional Systems of the Mammalian Brain," "It is our unique human tendency to dwell on, and hence to sustain, our emotional disturbances that casts a longer shadow on our mental life than is common in animals."

The human experience would be a grey and lackluster existence if not for the presence of our emotional states. They give us a sense of aliveness and are critical to our ability to make conscious choices about our lives. Our emotions tell us how we feel about the world around us. From joy to pain, we utilize our feelings to survive much like a lion might use his claws.

To quote Panksepp again, "During emotional arousal, actions guide perceptions while, during [cognitive activity], perceptions guide actions." When you have high activation such as distress or threat, the sympathetic nervous system comes online, creating chemicals to push us towards fight or flight. But when that threat is deemed inescapable or the stress becomes chronic, forcing the body to cope, the dorsal vagal comes online, providing a shut off system. When we live in emotional activation, our neurochemicals are doing the choice making. When we participate in SomEx^{SM}, we can begin to influence the effects of those neurochemicals. We are retraining the body to shift its response to external stimuli and, in turn, are creating a way to reprocess and resolve both past experiences and our reactions to life in the present moment.

When Cathy did her work around her sexual timeline, she was able to bring her emotions into clear view. As she explained later, "I didn't feel guided by my emotions; I felt as though I was guiding them. I stayed present enough that I could determine how the story was making my body shift in response, and I was able to pay attention and respond to those adjustments. It became a gentle process and not a reactive one."

For Cathy, reality was a hard and dis-regulated place, and she learned early on that fantasy was a controlled escape. Unfortunately that fantasy was coupled with the abuse; together, the two imprinted her sexual/relational template.

Now, child play and fantasy are both appropriate developmental processes that allow children to explore their imaginations. But for people who have lived in systems where fantasy becomes a mechanism for escape from abuse, the fantasy experience elevates or even intoxicates the emotional affect. The fantasy gets fused with the abuse and becomes entrenched with the person's thoughts and belief systems, creating an altered reality. It is in this reality that the Adaptable Self finds its identity.

Early in her work, Cathy shared with me a story about a rare gentle moment with her father:

> *We are moving to a bigger house. It is pink and two story. Susan and I will have our own rooms. We run to them. They are at the top of the stairs. Mine has a red carpet and a white bedspread. There is a closet with a door, and a large gray dresser with a mirror on it. Susan comes into my room, and we grab hands and start to squeal, jumping up and down. We hear Dad striding up the stairs. We stop and watch the doorway, waiting for him to appear. He is scowling and asks us, "What is going on?" I say nothing, but Susan can't help herself, explaining, "We are just sooo happy!" Her voice squeals a little and she gives a little jump. Dad laughs and smiles and puts a hand on each of our heads. He puts his arms around us and takes us over to window to show us the back yard. It is dark and the*

perfectly trimmed grass looks like velvet. I say so. Dad
pulls me closer to him and strokes my hair.

In Panskepp's book, *Archaeology of Mind*, he explains that there are seven emotional affects, which are primal or intrinsic to the human mind: seeking, rage, fear, lust, care, panic/grief, and play. He believes these affects can act independent of our thoughts, stemming from "our ancient neural networks" rather than our rational meaning making of life. It is these affect states that get altered in relation to stress or trauma, affecting the natural rhythm of our experience. As he writes, "It is hard for many to imagine that affect can exist independently of thoughts—that in their initial developmental form they are largely objectless states of mind which through various types of learning, come to imbue the material-cognitive world with values."

These values say that no matter how cruel one man can be, a moment of his kindness is worth a lifetime of romanticizing. Through the variable reinforcement of the trauma bond, Cathy lived in a random cycle of abuse and kindness. She never knew if the hand stroking her hair was about to cause injury or offer her love. She was caught between knowing that there was something wrong in her marriage yet believing that love was eternal. Many of us live in the paradox of this kind of messaging, always knowing that the pain of the relationship looms but hoping that love and fantasy will prevail.

The Adaptable Self thrives on this incongruence. Tossed between the waters of others' behaviors, it learns to negotiate away its values, passions, and identity, forming the veil that separates us from our authentic selves. If that veil were to fall away, we would no longer be able to live in the system that molded the Adaptable Self. We would either need to leave, or we would fail to survive. The Adaptable Self is at once our greatest obstacle and our strongest survival skill set, keeping us disassociated from the trauma.

Cathy had been hoping that one day her second husband Chris would come home and say, "You were right. You said this brilliant thing, or that brilliant thing, and I have realized the error of my ways. And I love you and I will be a different man for you. And I will never hurt you again."

And he would mean it. But that ain't life, and it certainly isn't love addiction.

Through SomEx^SM, we are healing the original lie. We are confronting the incongruences of the trauma bond, the one that created the attachment disorder in the first place, and we are repairing that deep chasm between what happened and how we have reacted to it.

Instead of living in the effects of trauma, we begin to live in the congruency of healing and repair. It's not easy work, and there are days where we have all felt stalled, when we said, "No way. I am done with this." But then the pain drives us back, and we lose hope that we can finally integrate our life story with that spirit behind the veil, the great resourced space that lies within us all.

BRAIN BASICS BY MICHELLE: MIRROR NEURONS, NEUROCEPTION & NEUROPLASTICITY

Somatic Trust cannot be built without safe and embedded neurological connections between people. As more work has been done to recognize and understand the way the brain works, we have begun to see that people can in fact be changed and, more importantly, that they are often changed by working with other people. For years, psychiatry believed that your neurological blueprint was set by the age of eight and there wasn't much that could be done after that, but what neuroscientists are discovering is that such psychological predetermination is a myth. The brain can create new neural pathways and does so by conscious behavioral modification and practice.

We begin this process by engaging our mirror neurons. This part of the brain is connected to the frontal lobe and is part of our primary brain organization, coming online within days of our birth. When babies are born, they do not yet have sight, but as soon as they begin to see, their mirror neurons begin processing and reflecting the world around them. To start, the brain takes information from the mother's face, beginning to pattern their own responses after her gestures and reactions. I have great video of my son and me doing this. He is three-months old and I am making faces at him as he tries desperately to make the faces back to me. There is the connection that is at once wordless and somatic, as he mirrors what he sees me doing, touching on those primary functions of the brain.

This is why the still face video was so disturbing for the child. Without a connection to mimic and mirror, the baby has no way to communicate back, and becomes deeply activated over the insecurity of the interaction. Even as adults, we experience this connection or lack thereof. We need to see that our emotions and behaviors are mirrored in those attached to us, recognizing feelings of empathy or distrust, and being able to identify the level of safety in our environment based on our ability to reflect and mirror its stimuli.

As we grow to recognize this process, we begin to engage more in neuroception, recognizing how we reflect the world and how the world is able to reflect back to us. When we begin to seek ways to repair from emotional rupture or dis-regulation, we are able to begin attuning to those around us. As a therapist, my job is to be well regulated in my reactions and dialogue with my clients. The left brain might be interested in my portrayal of thoughts and opinions, but the right hemisphere is identifying whether my actions and emotions are congruent—whether I am saying one thing and thinking another. That's a necessary piece around repair; we must begin to understand that we cannot be in regulated healthy attunement unless we are regulated ourselves. If we don't behave consistently with what we're neurocepting, we may only create further rupture, breaking those tenuous bonds of Somatic Trust. This is where the mirror neurons come online again. Because once you begin to create safety and attunement, people can start paying attention to what you're communicating to them and they can safely communicate with you.

Neuroplasticity is the brain's ability to form new neural coalitions that allow for repair, bringing change to the impaired. If you mirror empathy, you will be more likely to receive it whereas, if you mirror criticism, you will similarly find criticism. If you do the former in a deep enough practice, you begin to create new pathways in empathy and kindness, in regulation and respect. The safest and most effective place to begin that practice is in the therapeutic effort, where the therapist offers ongoing affirmative neuroception to their client as a means to create new neural pathways towards positive choice making. Then we get to see this work expanded at the group level where, as they often say in twelve-step fellowships, you allow the group to love you until you can love yourself.

Through these regulated relationships, we begin to develop new patterns. Here's the thing: you can't get rid of the old neural pathways, but you can start creating and choosing to take new ones. It's like going mountain biking. Sure, there are well-worn paths that are smooth and easy, but they're going to take you the same places you've always gone. If you want to create a new path, you need to be prepared for the bumpy ride because it's going to be rough and filled with weeds. While it's going to take some time to make the ground smooth going, with deep practice, you can begin to create a new network in your brain, grounded in a regulated arousal zone.

CHAPTER SIX

Somatic Intervention

Since the time of Aristotle, humans have tried to figure out how complex systems and patterns arise out of relatively simple interactions. Philosophers have long called this process emergence theory. In terms of somatic work, emergence theory helps us to explain how a group of people working together is more effective than one person trying to solve a problem on their own. This links us back to Somatic Trust where, once an empathetic, emotionally regulated bond is created between two individuals, they are able to better process trauma and affect healing. As a therapist, it's difficult to fake empathy because you have to be able to embody it. But in order to develop and embody empathy, one has to first look at his or her own wounded history.

This embodiment ultimately extends beyond the client-therapist relationship and into the larger community. In community healing, there is not a leader but, rather, an emerging presence of safety. This collective unconscious is implicit, vibrational, and organized even within its own chaos. It is greater than the sum of its parts. Once the SomEx^SM process progresses through the stages of attention, trust, and modifying behavior, we are then able to intervene on the barriers to resiliency by unlearning fixed action patterns and, in turn, creating healthy attachments. Like a school of fish or the flight pattern of a flock of birds, when we find that common spatial bond of empathy and resiliency, we are able to create a dynamic community that leads us where we want to go.

Welcome to group therapy. I often say being in group is like sitting in the room with the differentiated parts of your ego. These archetypes—the victim, the perpetrator, the martyr, the addict, the hero, and the scapegoat—are all brought together as separate parts that become united in the group experience. These archetypes begin to engage and co-mingle, creating an environment for transformation, but these aspects of ourselves are rarely recognized in isolation. It is by coming to understand the man who has cheated on his wife, by understanding the woman who was beaten by her father, by seeing the child inside a business executive and the Divine within a sex addict, that we can have compassion for those pieces of ourselves.

Regularly in our group sessions we have multiple perspectives of an issue brought together in a collective goal: to find healing despite what one's story might be. As the therapist, it is my job is to facilitate, to allow each client to have his or her own perspective and experience in the group process. Through that, they are better able to increase their awareness and expand their emotional constriction by engaging in and being open to other people's perspectives. Together, the group slowly learns to trust each others experiences and ultimately come to the place where they all have the opportunity to experience empathy for each other. It's much like the old Native American saying, "Don't judge a person until you have walked a mile in his moccasins."

"We became a family of choice"

For the Native American people, this belief was lived in their culture. The importance of "relation" was central to Native American spiritual traditions, as symbolized by the Circle of Life, which contained the basic elements of nature: fire, earth, water, and wind or, as defined by certain tribes, as spirit, nature, body, and mind. The sensory experience, or somatic experience, was not just a part of a therapeutic effort; it was a way of life. Native peoples believed that these elements existed in an involved system of interdependence, a dynamic state of harmony and balance.

This harmony was not only a key aspect of their culture; it was imperative for their survival. Through community rituals, indigenous people were able to support each other through their experiences and the expression of intense emotions, which allowed them to negotiate and survive painful conditions. This process was essential to restore innate instincts and usually involved rhythm, music, chanting, dance, expressions of art, healing touch, and ceremony. It is no surprise that when natives were brought into the European culture and were stripped of these important rituals, addiction and violence skyrocketed amongst their people.

Back before cell phones and grocery stores, communication and convenience were unused terms. Life was a perilous test between survival and death in which demonstrating one's needs and guaranteeing their realization was key to the survival of the species. Because of this, Native American traditions placed importance upon clan contribution and cooperation. They believed that in order for the community to be healthy, all members had to seek harmony with themselves, with others, and with their surroundings.

Today, we see this need for unity in response to both a public tragedy and public celebration. For example, we have seen these wide and emotional responses to shared tragedies whether in the aftermath of 9/11 or in the Boston Marathon bombing. People come together in times of great need, and out of that emergence comes an energy that before was unrealized. Whether in a twelve-step group or in group therapies, you get that same flow of life-affirming spirit that the tribes themselves used to experience. Just like the school of fish who swim together or the flock of birds migrating across the sky, people come together and find harmony in unity.

In group therapy, this coherence is key not only to the therapeutic effort but to each person's personal transformation. It took Cathy a while to begin to trust her group, but as she explains, it became a great source of empathy and comfort:

> *Our group was composed of sex addicts and co-sex addicts. I was in the room with male sex addicts, and though one would have expected it to be polarizing, it wasn't. In fact there was a really strong coherence between us. We would go out to dinner after almost every group. We became really close friends—there was so much honesty and openness amongst us. It took me a year to begin to trust—it became almost imperative for me to tell my whole story. At the time I wasn't thinking about it in those terms, but I was compelled to come clean in front of the group so that I could have some integrity. They had become my family of choice, yet I felt that I still wasn't sharing in the way that everyone else had come to do.*

This level of coherence between group members instills unity. If water seeks its own level, so honesty seeks its reciprocal. Therapy can create what is known as an earned attachment where the therapist can be a "good enough" model of caregiving until the client begins to experience relational safety and trust. Trauma patterns are about cohesion of neural pathways where there is rigidity in the emotional processing system, not unity. Group therapy brings people out of isolation and offers new neural bonding patterns, leading to coherence. Coherence is the natural flow and functioning of the neural experience where neuroplasticity is fostered and where trauma can be repaired.

Just as the Native Americans used to do, we reconnect with the tribe and we begin again to place importance upon clan contribution and cooperation, and an orientation toward living in the present. Group therapy can be a step towards the harmony that was once so key to our indigenous survival, and still is today.

Though we no longer need to forage or hunt for our food, or outrun predators from other species, and though most of us go to sleep and wake up in the same shelter, having an expectation that it won't be destroyed or moved the next day, we still experience the trauma of survival in other ways. We still experience the leftovers of primitive defense for which many of us were not allowed to utilize the survival skills we have been wired to use. When raised in abuse, we should be able to fight or flee, but often children are not allowed either option, instead being trapped in the cycle of shame and fear until they are able to do the work in adulthood to achieve the repair that was lacking in their family systems.

"An extremely brave thing"

One day in group, I asked that Cathy choose one of the group members she most trusted to do an exercise with her. Relaxing into the mutual trust that had developed between her and another member, she told the story of how one night her father came into the dining room and found their cat eating the food off the dining room table. In one fell swoop, he picked up the cat, throwing it out the back door. Though afterwards he cried and confessed that he had not wanted to kill the cat, an hour later the children found it outside, dead from a broken neck.

After Cathy shared, I asked if anyone else felt like they had some work to do. One of the other men in the group, Mark, a graphic designer in his early forties raised his hand. He explained that years before, in a drunken rage, he had beaten his dog. The grief and guilt permeated throughout his life as well as his core belief that he was a perpetrator.

I asked Cathy and Mark to face each other so that they could share how each experience made them feel. They held hands as each one expressed their fear, their panic, and their shame over the incidents. Connecting the archetypes of victim and perpetrator, they were able to share and engage together in an experience of reparation.

Finally, Mark reached out to embrace Cathy and she quickly accepted, holding him as they both began to cry, mourning the innocence lost due to the effects of rage and violence. As Cathy said later, "It was an extremely brave thing for Mark to do. By sharing his story, I got to mourn not only the loss of that cat but also the loss of my father's healing, which he never got to achieve. Instead, I got to see Mark experience his."

Relational trauma results in the chronic ruptures that accumulate and impair the nervous system's ability to develop resiliency. It is when a person with relational/developmental trauma is not offered reparation that their body's natural abilities are thwarted. Self-regulation can be enhanced when there are interventions on that ruptured relational/developmental template. For Cathy and Mark, they were able to foster new neural patterns based on safety and trust, and begin to reestablish how they could connect to others even in heightened states of activation.

We unconsciously perceive inner or external cues as to the safety, danger, or life threat in the present moment. We do this through our ability of neuroception, which enables us to:

1. Socially engage when safe,
2. Defend or withdraw when in danger, and
3. Freeze when we perceive our life is threatened.

In dangerous, life-threatening situations, high levels of neurochemical activation are necessary for survival, but they also disrupt the normal flow of these chemicals in the organism. If not discharged in defense or escape, this high activation becomes chaotic or is held immobile in a state of freeze. What I once thought was intensity and anger turned out to be a high state of fear and anxiety.

The healing comes when we realize we don't have to continue experiencing life through this constant state of chaos or freeze. SomEx^{SM} allows us to slow down and attune to our sensations, becoming conscious by utilizing neuroception. As Michelle previously explained, neuroception is a key communicator not only about what's happening in the body but also about what's happening in the environment around us. This is what links the lower brain activities (the body, what I pick up on the environment, my immediate ability to mirror the neurobiology of others) to the higher brain activities (linear thought and executive thinking).

I can be sitting across from a client, and though they may not be saying anything, I am able to employ my own neuroception to tap into the inner subjective field between us. These are the components of emergence theory that can be supportive of psychotherapy. With that awareness we are then able to consciously choose strategies regarding social engagement, creatively choosing our response to a given situation based on this body/mind awareness. Alternatively, we are able to understand when connections are being formed, when it's okay to trust. By tending to previous ruptures in trust, a co-created attention to the client's experience is developed, allowing for an embodied sensation of repair and healing. Other relational resources that aid in this mending can be group therapy, support groups, and participation in community.

SomEx^{SM} is grounded in this interpersonal neurobiology because it helps us identify these thwarted patterns to protect and defend. In offering one individual the opportunity to "help others alleviate suffering and move towards well-being," as Dan Siegel explains in *The Mindful Brain*, they are more able to experience personal empathy. Twelve step programs have used this model for decades—"One alcoholic helping another"—but now we have begun to have a better understanding of how this behavioral modification method can also lead to implicit healing. SomEx^{SM} allows us to heal the ruptures in trust created by relational trauma. Again, we don't wound alone and we don't heal alone.

The neural connectivity that can be created in group psychotherapy may be one of the fundamental ways in which therapy is able to affect neural activity. This is where, according to Siegel, collective consciousness is given the opportunity to harness, "neural plasticity by altering previously automatic modes of neural firing and enabling new patterns of neural activation to occur." That's why telling your story from a left-hemisphere narrative approach is not sufficient for repair of those ruptured places that are held frozen in the right hemisphere. In fact, when we just "tell" our stories we are not integrating them. Integration comes when we begin to have sensations around them.

For Cathy and Mark, they were able to establish empathy and compassion for one another, neurologically connecting around a shared experience by employing different perspectives. Through this work, they were able to experience repair around their individual ruptures, both created by unexpressed grief from their past. By co-experiencing and co-regulating this therapeutic process, they were able to achieve empathy where before there was only pain. This is one of the transformative goals of SomEx^{SM}.

"This is yuck…for all of us"

Eventually, Cathy did her entire sexual abuse timeline in two group sessions. We went as far as she wanted to go in the first session and then, the following week, we finished the work. Cathy had always had trouble watching the clock during her work. As she explained, "she didn't want to take up too much time."

I decided to take the clock down so she wouldn't be tempted to try to control the process but, rather, to actually have the opportunity to stay engaged in it. Before we did the work, she had expressed her issues around talking about her sexuality in front of sex addicts. Certainly, I understood. To trust people who had the same addiction as both her husbands was challenging but it was also a unique opportunity for Cathy to discern the different aspects of the addiction, tweezing apart the qualities that were hers versus those qualities of her husbands'. Through the work, Cathy would have the opportunity to see the differences and similarities between the addictive cycles.

In neurological terms, this discernment allows for an uncoupling of neural networks that have been firing together. These are the networks that have created ruptures in the natural patterns of one's neurochemistry. Processing and tweezing apart allows for this differentiation between these neural network patterns. By telling her story and remaining present in her body, Cathy began to experience the realization that her Authentic Self was not shaped by what happened to her. She didn't have to live in "victim" mode, believing that all men are perpetrators and that she would forever be the perpetrated.

Over the course of two group sessions, she explained how from the first day she was with Bill, he pressured her for sex. He demanded that she wear sexy lingerie even when she wasn't comfortable wearing it. As she explains, "Later I would always put that on if he was giving me the silent treatment so that I could feel some control over changing his behavior."

She told the story of finding out about Chris's pornography addiction and how, when she found out about his mistress, Chris didn't even make a false promise to leave her. "He acted as though it was a viable choice and that I should somehow be okay with it."

Over those two sessions, Cathy spoke about Chris's betrayal but also about the ongoing sexual violence and physical trauma from her first marriage. "I just wanted one day where I wasn't expected to have sex with Bill. One day where I could be free, but it felt like I was living in a prison. Though I tried to set boundaries, they always failed. Bill was my captor, and I was his hostage."

Throughout Cathy's story, I would ask that she pause and make eye contact around the room, focusing on someone she felt comfortable with, and then ask her to stretch outside of her comfort zone and also look at one of the sex addicts. In their eyes and in their faces, she saw the transformation beginning to happen for them as well. As they heard about the perpetrations, the pain caused by sex addiction, they could experience empathy for those they had harmed.

Whereas before, Cathy had been concerned how the men would react in group, telling me, "I don't want anybody thinking about me like that. It just feels so vulnerable and what if it's damaging to them, what if I am triggering their own issues?" she seemed ready to see what was on the other side of that fear.

When we work together in a co-regulated, therapeutically safe space, there's not much room for the triggers of addiction to thrive. Through this process of sharing and disclosure, Cathy strengthened her attachments with both the women and the men in the room. It is through these attachments that we begin to uncouple the neural networks that have bonded vulnerability together with betrayal. And in the process of relational repair and embodied disclosure, Cathy was creating the ingredients for new neural pathways to begin forming.

This level of Somatic Trust is about creating Somatic Empathy between individuals. The common definition of empathy is the ability to understand and share the feelings of another. The principles of neuroception are the framework for Somatic Empathy. It's not just about conscious analysis but, rather, becoming a conscious observer of what one feels in their own body.

As Cathy spoke, she was integrating the left hemisphere, retelling the story and connecting into its right-hemisphere sensory, energetic experience. When she was done, she turned around to look at the clock that I had previously removed—she hadn't realized it was gone the whole time. She explained, "It was a big victory that I didn't look at the clock until I felt finished. I burst out laughing when I noticed the clock wasn't there! The whole group applauded."

It took a while for Cathy to get to this place, but I knew she was not to be pushed. She had been pushed her whole life into doing things she didn't want to do. It was our job to protect her and to help her see that we could be trusted.

When we were done, I said to the group, "I want to hear how this is affecting everyone. By the expressions on your faces, it appears Cathy's story has had an impact on this room. I can see the tears in your eyes."

As the group members went around the circle, they all gave feedback to Cathy about their experiences hearing her story. As one client said, "Your story reminded me of some of my behaviors but only in the way they made me feel afterwards: sick, ashamed, and wishing I could behave differently."

In being able to associate to and co-regulate along with Cathy through her story, that man was given another empathetic resource. He could finally see his role in his own demoralization and that of the women in his life.

Cathy told me that she realized as they spoke, that love and sex addiction "is yuck… for all of us."

"I was able to see his side"

In the 1980s and 1990s, researchers working at the University of Parma in Italy discovered an interesting pattern in animal behavior. These neurophysiologists had placed electrodes in the ventral premotor cortex of the macaque monkey to study neurons specialized for the control of hand and mouth actions, such as taking hold of an object and manipulating it. During each experiment the researchers allowed the monkey to reach for pieces of food and recorded from a single neuron in the monkey's brain in order to measure the neuron's response to certain movements. They found that when the monkey saw a person pick up a piece of food, their neurons reacted in much the same way as when the monkey itself picked up the food.

In *Parenting from the Inside Out*, Dan Siegel and Mary Hartzell describe the effects of these neurons: "Mirror neurons are found in various parts of the brain and function to link motor action to perception. For example, a particular neuron will fire as a subject watches an intentional act of someone else, such as the lifting of a cup, and will also fire as the subject herself lifts the cup. These neurons don't merely fire in response to any action seen in another person. The behavior must have intention behind it."

This is where that still-face experiment comes in. There are hundreds of muscles in one's face by which we communicate social engagement through the ventral vagal system. But how do we communicate when our inner experience and outer expressions are incongruent?

I remember years ago when I caught myself yelling at one of my sons. My face was contorted with anger, but then I stopped myself and watched what his face was doing as he tried to make sense of mine. Internally, I was experiencing stress, but, externally, I was expressing anger. I was able to choose in that moment to soften my face and settle my internal activation to be more congruent. I watched his little face soften to match my own. This is the power of mirror neurons.

And it takes place in every small action we make with those around us. My son did not know how to process my expression, which was actually incongruent with my internal experience. When we do not know how to respond in a situation, we will either have to move into sympathetic arousal or dorsal collapse. Since that day, I have made a sincere effort to notice how I communicate in my relationships and in my family. Growing up, there was a lot of secret keeping in my home. We didn't communicate verbally; instead, I had to interpret facial expressions. My mother would just have to look at you to express disapproval. It is in these incongruences, between what is expressed and what is felt, that activation arises.

This is why coupleship work is some of the hardest work you can do because couples have a host of non-verbal and implicit ways in which they communicate with each other, often expressing their own unresolved traumas. Couples are attracted to each other to heal such rifts in their respective psyches. SomEx[SM] teaches us that before we react to someone else's communication, we first need to check inside to see if we are operating out of our own Optimal Arousal Zone. Due to the effects of mirror neurons, if I am unregulated, the other person is going to experience that as well whereas, if I am in a regulated place, it provides the opportunity for the other person to regulate themselves. I do this everyday when listening to clients' stories in order to create an environment of safety and trust, but when we are raised in abusive or volatile environments, we become unable to clearly read the communication of those around us. That trauma triggers a physiological arousal that affects and impacts our belief systems and, thus, distorts them. This process can be repetitive, creating an unconscious looping dynamic that can create both physical and/or mental health issues.

As therapy helps us to address this looping of our distorted thinking, we are able to incorporate elements of movement, motility, affect, and sensation in order to begin a renegotiation of previous belief systems. This is that uncoupling concept again where intrinsic qualities get coupled with traumatic experiences, such as vulnerability and betrayal. Just as in their shared experience of the abused pets, Cathy and Mark were able to renegotiate the experience of their childhood traumas and, in turn, create a more secure relational attachment thanks to neuroplasticity.

Again this isn't easy work. As Cathy explained, when she first entered group and began to hear other's experiences of sexual addiction:

> *It was hard to hear their stories. Not because it triggered my trauma, but because I found myself having such empathy for them. Though their stories were totally different from what I had experienced, I saw the pain on their faces, heard the regret in their voices, and could feel myself binding with their emotional awareness of the event. I related to one group member who was really reluctant to talk about the things that he had done to his wife in front of me because he was afraid that I would react. His wife was a lot like me, but rather than taking her side, I was able to see his side. I told him, "I am your wife." But because of that I could see how I acted and I was able to empathize with him.*

Years ago, I treated a divorced female client who at the age of sixty was just beginning to learn how to live. As a child, this woman's parents would have her go to her room immediately after school, only allowing her to come out for dinner. Once dinner was finished, she was sent to bed, even as early as 6:00 in the evening. She was sitting in session with me one day when she asked, "Tell me, Kent. What do you really think therapy is about?"

And I will say to you what I said to her: "I think it's about re-parenting."

For so many of us, the neurological communication that was mirrored to us did not give us the sense of safety we needed to navigate the world around us. The one thing so many addicts say when they come into recovery is that they did not have the rulebook in life. Even if their parents seemed to know what they were doing, it seldom felt communicated, and often wasn't.

Though verbally they may have been told what to do or how to live, often what was mirrored to them was a contradiction. This incongruence created a split between the inner experience and the outer reality. This chasm is what fuels emotional dis-regulation. Living outside of one's emotional arousal zone is created from that dissonance in the inner experience and outer expression. When someone is saying they love you but expresses disappointment and disgust in their facial expressions, one has little choice but to disconnect from their internal, intuitive experience. Therapy shouldn't be a blaming process because often our parents didn't intend to harm us. But at some point, we must be willing to re-parent ourselves.

It is through this re-parenting and re-negotiation of our stunted identity development that we are able to move into what is known as choice making. According to John and Linda Friel's book *An Adult Child's Guide to What is "Normal,"* "Codependency is a dysfunctional pattern of living which emerges from our family of origin, as well as our culture, which results in an arrested identity development and creates an overemphasis on the things on the outside of us, and under-emphasis on things on this inside of us." Codependency is an addiction process, but choice making is when we become responsible for our intentions and behaviors. As we begin to re-parent ourselves, we become more emotionally regulated in our own lives, and we have the opportunity to break the cycle of codependency.

As Cathy says about her own parenting today, "When my older children were growing up, there was a clear pecking order in the house. Bill was on top and then me and then the oldest child all the way down the line. That's how I controlled them. Today, I work really hard not to do that. I am much more apt to see what is going on with my kids and to find out what they need."

Once we are able to better regulate ourselves, the need to control others dissipates. We can see where we are mirroring shame and fear, where we are thwarting exploration and expansion of one's identity development. It is when we begin to live in the Optimal Arousal Zone that we allow for the attuning and attending to our own thwarted potential.

As Peter Levine writes in *Healing Trauma*, "When we're in trauma, we're not able to be in the present, to see, hear, smell, and perceive our immediate environments fully. As your nervous system begins to return to balance, your orienting responses will naturally begin to come back on line."

When we begin to become regulated in our emotional state, we are able to re-connect back into the world around us. As you go through your day, begin to recognize how you orient to the world around you:

- When you wake up, take a few moments to orient to your space and notice your environment and your experience of it. Feel the temperature, how your skin responds to it. Pay attention to anything you might notice either around you or inside of you.

- As you go out into your day, pay attention to the people around you and what happens to you internally as you integrate with the world. It can be as microcosmic as noticing your breath when you are driving or how your breath shifts when you're around others. Let all your senses come online. Utilize your sense of touch, smell, sound and taste to make your noticing more vivid.

- When you go to sleep, check in with your body. Is there soreness and tension? Do you feel relaxed and at ease? Review the day that just happened, recall any sensory experiences that stood out for you, and note what your reaction was to them.

As you begin to live in more emotional harmony, notice how much more present you can be in life and how that presence can extend beyond your morning meditation and right into all the experiences and relationships in your life. Pay attention to how you experience the world around you. Are you really listening to the people in your life? How do your senses respond to your environment? Are you noticing the people and places and sensations in your life? By connecting to others through our somatic experience, we deepen our attunement to them and, in turn, are able to create healthier attachments—ones we might have missed in our own childhoods. We get to re-parent ourselves, and through the work, we find out that the child within us is worthy of love and empathy.

BRAIN BASICS BY MICHELLE:
COHESION AND COHERENCE

O ften coherence and cohesion will be confused as the same thing, and not just because they sound the same. Cohesion is frequently mistaken for functional thinking and behaving, because it is so closely linked to the logic of survival. But the same qualities that we develop to survive on this planet do not always serve us in our ability to experience and process it. When the nervous system is forced to remain at a level of overstimulation due to threat or neglect, it will adapt itself to the neurochemical experience. Remember, what fires together wires together. The adaptability of the brain allows for those who experience shock and developmental traumas to cope and survive. This should not be mistaken for the optimal level of recovery that one can achieve but, rather, an adaptation to the stress levels and subsequent saturation of endorphins that flood the system.

When the nervous system is flooded with high levels of stress hormones, the left hemisphere often looks for ways to make meaning from the sense of overwhelm. The left hemisphere utilizes its rational, meaning-making devices to allow us a way to adjust to the sensation of high activation in the body. This experience of stress hormones creates an over-coupling in the nervous system. The chronic levels of activation lead to an ingrained neurochemical wiring that becomes a habituated phenomena. This can be similar to what can clinically look like rigid thinking or obsessive/compulsive thinking. Examples of emotional manifestations of this can be anxiety disorders or hyperactivity. The individual can function within a narrow Optimal Arousal Zone and, thus, does not experience the rhythm and fluidity that integration can provide.

Coherence is when the three parts of the brain (brainstem, mid brain and neo cortex) operate in harmony and rhythm with each other. Differentiation occurs to unbind the hyper and hypo arousal states that lead to over-coupling. With the utilization of resources, the balance of the sympathetic and parasympathetic systems is restored. The Optimal Arousal Zone experiences expansion and allows for the development and strengthening of resilience. Coherence is a more grounded, centered state that allows for choice making. The polysemantic ability of the right hemisphere (which is able to hold a number of theories) reduces the rigidity and ruminative nature of the over-coupling and provides an opportunity for an embodied experience of thinking, feeling, and behaving.

The over-coupling that leads to cohesion can be realigned in SomEx[SM]. Due to neuroplasticity and the brains ability to reorganize and rewire, the hyper aroused states can be treated and reduced with this cutting edge therapy. In slowing down the activation response and bringing into consciousness an embodied awareness, clients of SomEx[SM] take an important step towards creating a new pathway of neurons wiring together. Through that transformation, behaviors begin to change. Just as our biography is our biology, so our biology can also predict our futures. As we change our neurobiology, we are able to change how we feel, behave, and act in the world around us. Rewiring our responses for repair rather than rupture and connecting our choices with our Authentic self. When we do this, rather than the adaptability to which our neurons have been previously wired, people find that through this practiced awareness, not only do they change, but the relationships around them are forever altered.

PART THREE

Harmony

CHAPTER SEVEN

Somatic Practice

Dear Bill,

*You emotionally and sexually abused me for all of
our marriage. You lied to me, the Church leaders, and
to God about who you were when you married me. You
lied, tricked and manipulated me into marrying you
and then spent the rest of our marriage punishing me for
loving the person you were pretending to be. Every time
I said I loved you, you knew you were not the man I
thought you were. Every time I complimented you, you
knew you were a fake. Every time you used my faith
as an excuse for your abuse, you knew that you were
defying God. Why didn't you just tell me the truth?*

But the bigger question was why didn't Cathy just leave?
Simple. She had been groomed since birth to live in this state
of dissociation. When a person experiences attachment and shock
trauma, he or she develops dissociative gaps that obscure their
awareness of self and other, inhibiting healthy choice making.
Trauma not only constricts the neural pathways of our natural
inclinations for coherence and fluidity; it also constricts the
pathways to our Authentic Self.

We become dissociated from the reality of our lives. As Dr. Alan Schore writes, "dissociation is the result of the deficiency in psychological energy...Due to early developmental factors, the quantity of psychological energy is lowered below a critical point, resulting in the inability to bind and organize mental functions together in a whole self." In other words, the emotional energy it takes to merely cope diminishes one's ability to thrive. As Cathy explained to me later, "I could set boundaries, but I had absolutely no energy to uphold them. Someone would walk up to the boundary, and I would just lie down. It wasn't until I realized that I needed to practice having boundaries in order to keep them and to begin regulating myself in all my behaviors in order to have a life."

"I was going to clean it up"

In order for caregivers to accomplish a secure attachment bond, the primary caregiver must be able to regulate their emotional arousal and attune her own body to the infant's needs. That's how one assists a child in regulation. When a child is in a state of intense arousal without proper attunement, he or she will drop into a dorsal vagal state of dissociation. These states of dissociation will be held in the right hemisphere unless a safe caregiver offers repair. Over time, these states of dissociation create an inability to stay aware of the current lived experience. Part of my job is to help bring this awareness back.

Deep practice of these principles is the final step, and perhaps the most important step, in changing brain structure. Though not everyone at EHC has gone through a Reconstruction Day, most of them have had the chance to observe one, which can be almost as powerful. Reconstructions were developed in the 50s by Virginia Satir as a means of helping people have context and attention to their life narrative. At EHC, we weave into the Reconstruction

Day the language and elements of SomEx^{SM}, allowing the process to be a resourced and regulated investigation into trauma. The process is about looking at patterns and themes in the client's life so that they are given the opportunity to renegotiate the effects of trauma on themselves and their relationships. As I mentioned before, part of that practice may include the client sharing their biography, family genograms, journals, letters, and other personal background. In Cathy's autobiography, she shared the following story:

> *I was sweeping the floor. I was around eight, it was right after my baptism. I had this little fantasy going in my head that I was the "maid." I was going to do it wrong, and then re-enter and do it right. I swept the dirt under the kitchen rug as the incompetent maid, and my Dad walked in right at that moment. He backhanded me upside the head and asked me something like what did I think I was doing. I was paralyzed to explain it. I just said, "I was going to clean it up." He thought I was lying and hit me again.*

What would it be like not to live in the freeze and dissociative states created by abuse? What if we were given the tools to safely renegotiate the effects of such events? Lack of resolution around these events not only keeps us from enjoying our lived experience, it blocks us from discovering our Authentic Self. When Cathy froze that day in the kitchen, she not only detached herself from her truth, but also from that playful child within.

Many people aren't aware how their painful life experiences can be coupled with intrinsic traits or qualities that then get thwarted in developmental or attachment trauma. This coupling of our traits with prior pain is what we attempt to tweeze apart with the therapeutic process. I had a client with whom I was doing some somatic therapy, and I asked her to think of a resource that would be a safe place for her. She chose her grandchildren but as we began the work, she said that the idea of them was activating her too much. In the work, she became aware that her feelings about her grandchildren were coupled with her shame around her parenting when she was in active addiction. What evolved in the work was an awareness of how she spoils her grandchildren as a means to overcompensate and alleviate the guilt she has about own her parenting. This is one benefit of somatic attunement to the body. We can recognize where our current actions are coupled with unresolved issues from our past.

Through this deep practice, we use oscillation between a safe resource and the places of activation in order to renegotiate the effects of trauma. Through this practice of oscillation, we are able to develop new neural pathways that allow for change, and the deep practice of these states allow for a more myelinated neural pathway, which enhances one's self-awareness. We intuitively know how to handle situations that used to baffle us.

For many years, Cathy was so dissociated from her own lived experience that she had little awareness around the patterns in her life. She simply repeated those patterns that she brought from her relationship with her father into her relationships with other men.

But those patterns can be changed through deep practice, a co-created process whereby the therapist and the client enter into a shared experience that facilitates change. It is in the inner subjective space of a safe therapeutic relationship where the client is able to begin re-connecting to consciousness, memory, identity, and behavior. We honor that people do the best they can with what they have. This is not about denying someone their coping skills; it is about fostering a climate of curiosity where they can develop and employ new skills and begin to form healing relationships in the process.

"My choices do make a difference"

The famed psychologist Carl Jung believed that this new self-awareness leads to "a new synthesis of personality...taking into account those parts of the whole which have been neglected."

For Cathy, living in that Adaptable Self prohibited the synthesis of her personality. Her Adaptable Self created these coping skills, which became patterns throughout her life. Once Cathy began to have awareness around those parts of herself that had been neglected, she embarked upon a new sense of choicefulness. As she told me, "I'm not helpless anymore, and I've begun to realize that my choices *do* make a difference. I'm not dissociating away from my ability to make good choices, and I can take the next right step, or I can refuse to take it, and I can still let go of the outcome and know that another choice will happen for me."

This is why it's imperative to make conscious the unconscious in the therapeutic process.

These transformations do not take place over night; in fact, they a demand a concerted and ongoing effort. When Cathy called me to say she wanted to participate in a Reconstruction Day, I knew that the deep practice was working. This was a woman who had not even wanted to tell me her story, much less reveal it in front of a group of people.

As she explained when she made the decision, "I want for myself lights turned on in the areas that I am unconsciously keeping dim. My goal in therapy has always been to become aware of my traumas and trauma responses, and to consciously choose a healthier, happier life by purifying my intentions in every action and reaction."

She had already changed so much from that woman who walked into my office frazzled and fearful that she was going to lose another husband. I understood that her therapeutic effort had taken her to the place where she was finally ready to engage in those areas that had been kept "unconsciously dimmed."

By now, she was in a recovery group called Sex & Love Addicts Anonymous, and had even begun to sponsor other women with similar stories. She had acquired a sense of community through her group therapy, the twelve-step process, and the meetings to which she was a regular and committed member to both.

Sex and love addiction manifests as a sexual relational template that is coupled with trauma. In her deep practice, Cathy was able to experience an uncoupling of her relational sexual template from her years of trauma. She had enrolled back in school, hoping to become a writer, a dream she had never had the opportunity to fulfill. She began writing grants for some of the local charities in her town, receiving for the first time in many years a paycheck with her name on it. The interesting thing is that by the time the day of her Reconstruction arrived, though she and Chris were still working on whether to divorce, he had long stopped being her focus.

"I had been living in an emotional corset and now I was finally taking it off"

When someone suffers from such chronic states of dissociation, the personality will tend to fracture. It is in these fractures, that the Adaptable Self is emboldened. In situations where we are not emotionally safe, the Adaptable Self helps us to survive, disssociating from the legacy of pain and shame that many people bear from their family systems.

For me, the Adaptable Self allowed me to live in two worlds. In one of those, I got good grades, went to church, and was popular. In the other, I was using, drinking, lying, and living in sexual secrecy in an attempt to dissociate from the pain and shame of my own family.

Cathy had spent most of her adult life with her heels dug into this Adaptable Self. So had I. Every choice I had made as a teenager was to support this side of my thinking: get good grades, make people laugh, join the band, be popular. I was driven by the outward control I could assert over my "normalcy." For Cathy, it was to be loved and protected by a man.

As I have explained, the right hemisphere is unable to process trauma without emotionally regulated attachments. Instead, the left brain comes on and begins to rationalize and minimize the abuse or events that led to the trauma. The Adaptable Self is created and reinforced by the left hemisphere's need for meaning making. Without the tools for trauma reparation, the Adaptable Self will normalize surroundings that would be typically described as abnormal.

It is from this unconscious dance between the emotional parts of our experience and the Adaptable Self that we are offered a way to manage unbearable sensations and emotions. But through the discovery of an Authentic Self, we are finally able to create an alternative, providing an intrinsic resource for the person to deconstruct that Adaptable Self.

For Cathy, that work was ultimately what led to her Reconstruction Day. Two months before she came to me to request one for herself, she went to a Reconstruction for a group member, Mark, the man who once beat his own dog in a drunken rage.

In one of the sculpts, Mark developed an idea of what he wanted for his future, one that included a wife and children, a happy home, and a productive and successful life. To amplify this imagery, we surrounded Mark with role players representing his past traumas. These role players held one end of a long rope. On the other end were images of recovery he had identified. The role players representing his past offered messages that echoed his fears and shame while the role players representing his recovery offered affirmations. Mark was caught between the two sides of this sculpt and finally asked for help in order to move towards the future he had so clearly envisioned for himself. Cathy was one of the people who joined in helping Mark claim his recovery.

"It was like I was watching Mark's fingers be peeled from his trauma, and I realized how much of a grip I still had on mine. I didn't want to let it go, I didn't want to move forward. I didn't want to feel."

As Cathy joined to help Mark, she realized she was claiming recovery for herself. She wanted to be reconnected with her Authentic Self and to finally surrender to the process of a Reconstruction Day. I still remember looking over at Cathy in that moment. I could see the determination on her face. Clearly something was shifting in her somatic experience.

"I didn't get it right away, but in the months after Mark's work, I began to see where I was setting intentions and moving towards them without being helpless, without feeling out of control. And then I asked for the Reconstruction Day and began to notice changes in my behavior. My whole life, I had been living in emotional constriction and now I began to have the space to breathe more and to be myself."

The Authentic Self is fostered in our relational connections with others, those who mirror our inner worlds. One of the goals of somatic integration is to provide a safe container and therapeutic relationship for the client to begin to recognize their worth. When we begin to work out of that Authentic Self, the spectrum of our choices begins to change. We no longer have to live in the unconscious habits of the Adaptable Self but can live in choiceful awareness, inspired by the Authentic Self.

"We danced to the Age of Aquarius"

When someone commits to the Reconstruction Day, they are committing to bringing out the context of their story in all its texture and vibrancy and vividness. In one powerful display of trust, they share their stories with other members of the group and others from the recovery community. Often previous

Reconstruction participants, or "stars" as we call them, attend in a spirit of support and affirmation. It is the combination of these people—some of whom will be from one's small group therapy, some from family and friends, and others who have participated in Reconstructions before—that will become the Reconstruction "star's" orchestra.

In the Reconstruction Day we are mindful to present sculpts and information that help the star in their transformation without threatening their safety or sense of security in the group. As much as this work is about transparency, it is also about repair. Therefore the materials used in the Reconstruction Day are offered as a way to enhance and amplify their experience.

Ultimately, it is in this act of deep practice that the integration of the left and right hemispheres allows the person to explore their own potential. They develop awareness of where they lack emotional harmony and where they can begin to foster wholeness. In *Another Chance,* Sharon Wegscheider-Cruse developed the Wholeness Wheel as a means to express the possibility of human potential. In it, she offers six potentials of self that we can begin to achieve once we start integrating towards authenticity.

The first of these is our physical potential. Are we maximizing our physical potential by participating in self-care behaviors? In tracking this potential, we begin to examine:

- What does your body care and physical health look like?
- Do you have a healthy meal plan?
- Do you get regular exercise?
- Do you participate in hobbies and activities that engage your body?
- Do you maintain your physical and medical health care, i.e. getting checkups and physicals?

By the time Cathy had made it to Reconstruction Day, she had improved noticeably in her physical care and well-being.

She had begun walking every morning, paying attention to her physical health. She shared that she was more comfortable with her body, and was more comfortable in offering affection to her children and others. After years of sexual trauma, she was finally learning to become comfortable in her own skin.

So I knew that to open her Reconstruction, it was good for her to be reminded of this. In Cathy's autobiography, she wrote to me about an experience she had in grade school:

> *When I was in fifth grade, we were sent to a progressive religious school in Dallas. My teacher there was called Jesse, and he brought his dog to school called Sunshine. This was the early seventies. We didn't have desks and instead would sit on the floor and work at coffee tables and on beanbag chairs. There was a festival of some sort and our class did a big parachute dance with a real tie-dyed parachute, and we danced to "Age of Aquarius." I remember running under that canopy and the music filtering through the air, and I felt so alive. I felt so free.*

I saw this as an opportunity for Cathy to reconnect with a fun and playful resource from her past, so we opened up the day of her Reconstruction by unrolling a large parachute, and lifting it into the air. We played the song "Age of Aquarius" as the participants took turns running underneath the parachute, something that evoked a positive resource for many of them. Cathy appeared relaxed as she laughed, running underneath the fabric and reconnecting to that innocence of her childhood. She caught my eye and smiled. When Cathy first showed up at my door, she was a frazzled shadow of a woman. Now she was in celebration of her life. She had learned to dance.

"I feel a cold ball of something in my stomach"

As we moved through Cathy's Reconstruction Day, I decided that in the next sculpt we should look at a story she had told to me early on, one in which her world view was coupled with abuse and shame. When Cathy was only eight, she discovered that she couldn't hide the abuse in her family.

> *Policemen come to our classroom and talk to us. They are very nice. They talk to us very kindly. They say we should not be afraid of them. They are helpers. One of them is named Frank. I think he is handsome. A few weeks later Frank comes to our door. He asks Patty where our parents are. They are out. Patty is babysitting. Patty's eyes are wide and her face is pale. I try to tell her it's okay. He is a helper. He asks us all how old we are. I tell him that I know him, that he talked to my class. I call him Frank. He does not look at me and does not seem to hear me. I feel a cold ball of something in my stomach and I want to cry.*
>
> *Mom and Dad come home. They are angry. Why did Patty let the baby cry like that? Why did the neighbors call the police? If we kids would behave, the police would not come to our house. Now the whole neighborhood thinks we are neglected. I do not know what neglected means, but I feel ashamed. Maybe that's why Frank ignored me.*

For so many of us who were raised in painful or neglectful homes, we were never allowed to process those confusing events. We lived with a cold ball in our stomach, which is the body's way of holding the emotional contents of these events. In order to reach our emotional potential, we must be able to repair these unresolved somaticized feelings. We must be willing to discover where and how we are unable to express our emotions on a daily basis. As you look at your own emotional potential, ask yourself:

- Do you feel at ease with a full range of feelings?
- Do you express them openly and appropriately?
- Do you have a safe environment in which to talk about how you feel?

For Cathy, she had never been allowed to feel at ease, to express or appreciate her own feelings. In her Reconstruction Day, we did a sculpt of that night the police came to the door. Members of the group portrayed Cathy's siblings while someone else played Cathy as a little girl and two other group members portrayed the police officers. Cathy was able to watch this sculpt from the sidelines. I asked the role players to pause as I asked Cathy to look at her little girl self. "Cathy," I asked, "what do you see when you look at her?"

She replied, "I had wanted the policemen to see me. I wanted them to talk to me."

"Yes," I replied. "Now, I want you to look at that little girl over there and see how scared she looks. Are you able to connect with the feelings she might have had that night?"

Cathy breathed in. I could see the emotion pass over her. There was a shift in her facial expression as the memories began to surface. I encouraged Cathy to go very slow and gently into these held memories. We continued in this sculpt until she began to feel the cold ball in her stomach shift into unexpressed sadness and fear. Cathy stood up and walked to the group member portraying her little girl. They embraced as those long-held tears were finally released.

"She put her head on my shoulder"

When Cathy sent me her goals for the Reconstruction, she said that one of the things she wanted to look at was her shortcoming as a parent. For Cathy, she had two primary experiences in parenthood: one with her older ones—who were raised when she was in relationship with Bill—and the younger kids, who were still in elementary school when they first separated. These younger children had experienced a different mom, one who was recovering and choosing healthier behaviors, but Cathy still had a lot of guilt around her older children, most of whom had found similar behaviors of addiction and/or codependency.

Of Cathy's daughters, she had felt particularly bad for Megan. Much like Cathy's sister Patty, Megan had been the oldest of the children and was often asked to play the role of second mother. She filled in for Cathy in various ways, particularly when Cathy's addiction to Bill kept her from being emotionally available. It was Megan who would tend to her siblings and try to console them when they witnessed the consequences of their parents' sex and love addiction. When it came time for Cathy's Reconstruction, it was Megan who chose to attend.

A significant part of the reconstruction process is when we are able to repair damaged relationships. It is through this social engagement that we are able to reveal more of our Authentic Self. In looking at your own social potential, let's see what level of relationship building you are creating in your life:

- Have you found and developed a Family of Choice—three to five people who love and support you in your recovery process?
- Do you participate in activities that you keep you engaged with others, as opposed to living in isolation?
- Are you able to be your Authentic Self in social situations?

169

Before Cathy's Reconstruction, we agreed that she needed to write a letter of amends to Megan. During her Reconstruction Day, I invited Cathy and Megan to share the letter with the group. Mother and daughter sat together as Cathy read her words to her firstborn. Here is what she wrote:

> *Dear Megan,*
>
> *I want you to know how much your support in my recovery has meant to me. Your willingness to be honest and to confront me, and your readiness to forgive makes this easier for me. I cherish the relationship that we have now. It is one of the best joys of my life.*
>
> *I deeply regret being the kind of mother I was to you for most of your life. I set out to be a very different mother from what I ended up becoming. When you were newly born—and really, for the first several years of your life—I think I was a pretty good mother. I listened intently to you, and every question you kids asked, I answered as thoroughly as I could. We had really fun conversations, and I wrote some of them in my journal. I took you to the park, and played with you and pushed you on the swings. I danced with you, and held you on my lap, read to you, and sang silly songs with you. I supported and encouraged you in your interests.*
>
> *When you were about six is when things really started to change. I remember when you noticed a difference. You said that I had become an I-don't-know Mom. You said I used to tell you things and now I just said, "I don't know" to everything you asked.*
>
> *I knew I was failing you kids in many ways, and knew what I wanted to do differently, but I felt unable to sustain a change for any length of time. I know that I was very remote and unavailable.*

I know you took on a lot of responsibility at a young age. You were always interested in doing grown up things, even as a tiny child. I think this wouldn't have been such a bad thing if you had also received the attention and nurturing you needed and deserved. I made the mistake of viewing your interest in mature things as maturity and letting that be an excuse for treating you like an adult who had no need for mothering.

I love you so much. I have always loved you as best I could. Unfortunately, my best was only when you were young. I was woefully inadequate. You deserved so much more than you got from me. I am sorry I couldn't give it to you.

I am grateful for recovery and for what we have between us now. I am grateful that I can be really present in your life now. I am proud of the amazing woman you are, and I am hopeful for the children in your life, who will get so much more from you than you got from me.

I love you,
Mom

As Cathy read the letter to her daughter, Megan leaned into her. It was as though the rest of the room had disappeared, fading into the background of their shared life history, the intimate space held between mother and daughter. As Cathy told me later, "As Megan put her head on my shoulder, I could feel us being healed. Here we were, just the two of us, building that bridge between who we both had been and who we hoped to be."

We all have to start somewhere. For Cathy, she started with Megan. From there, she began to practice more healing in all of her relationships.

"I started pulling my inner child toward me"

Most people who come into therapy are pretty smart, but if clever and smart could get us better we'd already be better. It's really in that right-brained, body-based approach that we can re-claim those parts of ourselves that have been exiled or relegated to compartments. By integrating the left and right hemispheres, we begin expanding our mental potential as well as our ability to learn from the past and to envision a better future. This is where addressing cognitions, the process by which we acquire knowledge, allows us to explore our mental potential:

- Are you able to use past experiences as a way to change or alter current behaviors?
- Are you able to share and accept feedback regarding your thought patterns or decision-making?
- Are you able to foster a life that has creative intention and goal setting in it?

On Cathy's Reconstruction Day, we chose to do a sculpt that addressed her shame-based, irrational beliefs about herself. We had role players represent the various men in her life that had been abusive or neglectful to her. In the scene, someone representing Cathy's inner child was cowering behind "the men." Cathy's "inner child" held onto one end of a long piece of cloth. I then gave the other end of the cloth to Cathy and asked her what she wanted to do.

The group members representing the abuse in Cathy's life offered and echoed the irrational messages and beliefs that had shaped her mental framework. Cathy began to pull on the cloth, bringing her inner child out of from behind those messages. While she did this, she was asked to counter those irrational messages with ones that were based in her recovery, fostering a new belief system that allowed for creativity and hope for future.

"I don't want to be put in a box"

In twelve step programs, there is one line that either comforts people or freaks them out: "Made a decision to turn our will and our lives over to the care of God as we understood him."

Our spiritual life can be diversely defined but is integral to the whole self. Having a spiritual life has as much to do with values as it does with one's concept of God. Through our belief systems, we define our selves, and how we experience those selves in relation to the world and others.

Much like the Native Americans once believed, these spiritual elements not only put us in contact with the environment around us, they allow us to better connect with our families and communities. As you look at your own spiritual potential, ask yourself:

- Do you feel like you have a sense of purpose in your life?
- Have you been able to develop a set of values that resonate with your Authentic Self?
- Are you able to have compassion and non-judgment for yourself and others?

Cathy had had such a rigid spiritual system her whole life that revolved around her religious upbringing. This religious system constricted her ability to access her feelings and intuitions. The work of developing a spiritual system is not necessarily about religion but rather about incorporating a more expansive spirituality in the body. Cathy now calls herself a "Baptist hippie" because she has learned to balance her views and beliefs with those of her faith. As we were preparing for Cathy's Reconstruction Day, she came to me with some concerns that people might judge her for her religious beliefs.

Though worrying about what others thought didn't need to be her concern, I also knew that this was a woman who had fought hard for her views within the church. So many people ask me why I have chosen to live in Memphis. As an openly gay man with two adopted bi-racial children, I certainly could have lived in more accepting communities, but as I always explain, I wanted to be the one who stayed. It is one thing to walk out of an intolerant environment; it is another thing to change it from within. I know we might be well received in other places, but then where does that leave the young gay man like me, growing up in the South and desperately looking for a role model for the life he wants to lead?

Cathy made the same choice in her life. She could have left her faith, turning her back because of resentment and intolerance, but she wanted to be the one who stayed. Now that doesn't mean that decision is right for all of us. Some will need to leave their current environments in order to heal, but we get to make that choice in our recovery. We can reclaim our spiritual potential based on our truest beliefs and not necessarily on what was given to us.

"Fear was not real"

The goal of SomEx^SM is to help make the unconscious conscious in order to create opportunities for real choice making. As we begin to re-organize the Authentic Self with the Adaptable Self, a new internal strength emerges. We are able to be a conscious observer our lives while working within our Optimal Arousal Zone. In doing so, we reduce the likelihood of reacting to life from a hypo or hyper-aroused state.

Cathy had long fallen victim to the abusive or neglectful behaviors of those around her and was unable to claim her own Authentic self in those relationships. Instead, she had lived in various dissociated states, compartmentalizing the abuse and constricting any possibility for healing or change.

In her Reconstruction, I tried to help her see what little choice making she was actually able to do her in life. In one of the sculpts, we utilized some of the other group members to act as representatives of Cathy's church, specifically, the church leaders who kept encouraging Cathy to return to her husband, and in turn, to the abuse. In addition, I asked another member to role-play her husband Bill and two others to role-play Cathy's parents in order to demonstrate how her early life experiences had also groomed her to be submissive to the church followings. Through those messages, Cathy was never encouraged to make conscious choices for herself; instead she was taught to follow the rules and dogma of the church authority figures. Out of this, Cathy learned to be that submissive partner who could adapt to the abuse because eventually her husband, her family, and her church all perpetuated the same message. We used a prop of a dog collar that I asked the "Church leaders" to hold, which was attached to a leash which was then held by the group member playing Bill. Both props were being utilized for Cathy to see these symbols of her submission.

Cathy was watching from only a few feet away as she stood next to me. I looked over to see how she was responding. At first, I thought she was crying but then I realized, Cathy was chuckling as she shook her head.

"Are you okay, Cathy?" I asked.

She replied, "It's a little over the top, Kent. Don't you think?"

This woman had been living attached to a dog collar and leash nearly her whole life but, somehow, she thought the sculpt was overdramatized. Often, there is this moment in a Reconstruction and in life itself—that moment when we say "No fucking way." These are the moments in which deep spiritual surrender can take place and transform someone's life.

I turned to her. "We've haven't even started talking about what's over the top here, Cathy." Cathy began to challenge me as being ridiculous.

I had long been aware that Cathy's adaptability allowed her to use humor as a means to cover her real feelings. Many of us do. I continued talking, moving forward by making eye contact with Cathy as I gently explained, "Cathy, you have been looking to get help for years, and the very people you went to for help, sent you right back into abuse. You spent your whole life being the good Christian girl who can't get mad at her parents and who can't get mad at the Church and who can't get mad at anything. At some point your own religious abuse becomes your addiction."

I lowered my voice to nearly a whisper so Cathy could feel safe and heard.

"Abuse is imbedded in a habituated way. Being an addict feels so much more powerful than being the victim. You were groomed and set up for it. You believed your body and your sexuality to be sacred and you gave them to men who you thought would hold you in reverence, and that group set you up to be perpetuated for the next twenty years."

Finally, Cathy's smile disappeared. The weight of the moment, and the reality of the sculpt, was reflected in her facial expressions. I sat down across from her and gave her some tissues. I whispered to her, "It's all tangled up in there."

I continued, "Everyone in that picture has been a part of your abuse. Can you see that?"

At that moment, Cathy sadly nodded her head, and her expression began to look more congruent.

We put an elastic band around the perpetrators and another group member who was role-playing "Cathy" to symbolize the trauma bond. I asked members of the audience to begin to offer affirmations to Cathy that encouraged her to break free from the perpetrators. We then offered Cathy a rope that was connected to the group member playing herself, and I asked her what did she want to do with this picture.

Cathy then stated, "I want to get her out of there."

In doing so, Cathy was making an embodied conscious choice to break the trauma bond.

Sometimes, healing doesn't take place in one short event but over a space of time. Still, even healing needs a starting point and, as Cathy described later, that moment was hers:

> *It felt like no one else was in the room. I don't remember what you said to me after that, but I had this moment where I had this complete belief that there was nothing to be afraid of ever again. It was this incredibly pure moment where fear was not real. Up until that moment, I had lived my life afraid, waking up every morning with anxiety, but even now, when I think about that moment I can remember how it felt. It is my resource. It is that deep touchstone of somatic work that still allows me to breathe and stand in my place.*

It is conscious choice making that allows us to live in our Authentic Self. As you look at your own life, when have you had a glimpse of yourself as you really are? Perhaps one of those moments when you have listened to music, read a piece of poetry, or watched the sun rise. Amplify that glimpse into an image and begin to notice where that awareness is present in your life. Ask yourself:

- What resources can help connect you to your Authentic Self?
- Are you willing to seek guidance and be teachable?
- Do you cultivate any kind of practice that enhances the development of your Authentic Self?

Start seeing how this Authentic Self can be embodied in your choice making. Today, I am a proud gay man and parent. I wake up most mornings with a restored level of consciousness and clarity, allowing me to a better parent and therapist. That's a pretty long distance from the man who contemplated jumping off a bridge. But I would ask you to have some compassion for that part of you too. In many ways, that Adaptable Self saved us, but now I encourage you to see where it no longer serves you. As Victor Frankl once wrote, "Between stimulus and response, there is a space. In that space is our power to choose our response. In our response lies our growth and our freedom."

CHAPTER EIGHT

Building Relationships

D o you remember the old Charlie Brown cartoons where Charlie would run up to kick the football only to have Lucy remove it from his path every time? Sadly, many of us have lived our whole lives like Charlie Brown, believing that Lucy would do it differently this time. We get trapped in these fixed action patterns of behavior long past the point of them serving us. I wish that wasn't the case. I wish it wasn't for you or for me. But pain is a great motivator for growth, and is often a necessary condition in order to create change.

Cathy's life was driven by many of her own fixed action patterns. There was little room for intuition or imagination. Those patterns perpetuated her suffering and buffered her from her own intuition and choicemaking. Once she was able to start making healthier decisions, she had to start looking at what her new relational/sexual template might look like. She had to begin re-defining what relationships could mean and how she could begin to form healthy attachments with those around her. In *Erotic Intelligence*, author Alexandra Katehakis describes the steps to healthy dating. The first step is to consider your behaviors and identify the warning signs and deal breakers of both your own and the other person's behaviors. Some of the examples of boundary breaches in relationship development include diminishing your social circle or compromising your work, rationalizing your own or another's behavior, or behaving sexually before becoming emotionally connected. One of the other steps is to evaluate your partner's behaviors and look for signs that can re-enact your trauma, such as devaluing your personal growth, being emotionally or sexually non-monogamous, or having other untreated active addictions. These can all be a set-up for love addiction. The ability to face these truths and to make these choices doesn't come all at once, and we certainly struggle with them no matter how many years we've been doing this work, but what they allow us to do is to finally build healthy relationships in all areas of our lives.

"It still takes me longer than fifteen minutes but I'm getting there"

According to psychologist M. Mathew, "The body is an instrument of physical processes, an instrument that can hear and see, touch, and smell the world around us. This sensitive instrument also has the ability to tune into the psyche; to listen to its subtle voice, hear its silent music and search into its darkness for meaning." We can all have access to sensation and intuition. It is through this understanding that we come into wholeness with those around us. But when we come from a traumatized background, this "sensitive instrument" becomes impaired and its basic regulation is disrupted. The body is unable to experience coherent relational patterns.

Through SomEx[SM], we are able to better engage and attend to one another's needs, as well as our own. This mutual awareness allows for the repair of attachment wounds by creating a "shared rhythm" and experience between two or more people. It is in this fellowship that we can begin to develop more complex relationships. As the promises of Sex & Love Addicts Anonymous offers, "We will regain control of our lives; We will begin to feel dignity and respect for ourselves; Love will be a committed, thoughtful decision rather than a feeling by which we are overwhelmed and; We will relate to others from a state of wholeness."

I remember a number of years back when Cathy called me one day in a twit. She had just completed her sex timeline and unfortunately one of her group members Leslie was not able to be present. Leslie had called Cathy after her last session and asked if Cathy would tell what happened and what she shared with the group.

To Cathy's credit, she explained that she wasn't comfortable doing that. The woman pressed Cathy for a synopsis, but again Cathy responded no. She got off the phone in a huff and immediately called me, but I was busy with other clients and wasn't able to get back to her immediately. When I did, she had already calmed down.

She laughed, "Well, it still takes me five hours to get over something."

I told her how recently I had had an exchange with a colleague that started as a friendly argument but ended in a heated debate. That old codependent tendency surfaced in me, and before I knew it, I had stormed out of the room and back to my office.

The thing was this: I knew I was wrong. And though I had to sit with it for a moment, fifteen minutes later, I was able to go back in, apologize, and clarify my thoughts.

As I told Cathy, "After twenty-five years of recovery, if I can get it down to fifteen minutes, that'll just have to be good enough."

This work is about progress, not perfection. The left brain commands a more linear, perfectionistic life script whereas the right brain allows for flexibility and variation. The right brain is able to tolerate messiness, and intimate relationships are messy. Life itself is messy. We can create all the expectations we want, but, ultimately, joy comes in being able to accept that messiness. Because no matter how long or how well we do this work, we will never be perfectly attuned at all times. We will never live entirely without relational or emotional dis-regulation. That's not life. That's not being human. And to think that way puts us back in that rigid place—it puts us in cohesion rather than coherence. Coherence allows us to be as present and regulated as we can be, but when rupture moves us out of that coherent place, we quickly forget that repair is possible. Healing is available to us whenever we are willing to participate in the process of recovery.

Through this deep practice and awareness, we find that we intuitively begin to move away from those old insecure attachments, the ones that only led to recurring anxiety and stress, and we start building secure attachments, maintaining social engagement despite life's challenges and confrontations. It is in these attachments where intuition thrives, where we are able to relate spontaneously out of our Authentic Selves.

For years, I have used a prop of a hula-hoop to represent one's personal space and boundary. Clients are asked to stand to inside the hoop and somatically imagine having their own personal space. I ask them, "What's going to happen if you maintain your boundaries and don't sacrifice your personhood to meet others' expectations?" In secure attachments, we don't need to leave our hoop, and we can be strong enough to say that our hula-hoop means more to us than the demands of the other people in our life.

Recently, I was speaking with Cathy, and she told me, "It still takes me longer than fifteen minutes but I'm getting there."

"I see my children as people"

At birth, a baby's brain is rich with neurons. From that initial development, those neurons begin to build deep connective networks through their experiences of the world and their primary attachments. Interpersonal neglect and trauma affects the baby's ability for the brain development by inhibiting the growth of connectedness between neurons and sub-units of the brain. Neglect and trauma rupture the developing brain and leads to fragmentations, impeding integration of the developing self.

I know that I have done my best to raise two adopted sons in a prejudiced environment, but I also know that one day I might very well be sitting on the couch next to them across from someone who does what I do for a living. In our group room, we have a poster that says to me all the promises I hope to keep for my sons. I read it frequently, and now offer it to you. It reads, "As I grow, please…

- Understand that I am growing up and changing very fast. It must be difficult to keep pace with me but please try.
- Listen to me and give me brief, clear answers to my questions. Then I will keep sharing my thoughts and feelings.
- Reward me for telling the truth. Then I am not frightened into lying.
- Pay attention to me, and spend time with me. Then I can believe I am worthwhile.
- Do the things you want me to do. Then I have a good, positive role model.
- Trust and respect me. Even though I am smaller than you, I have feelings and needs just like you.
- Help me explore my unique interests, talents and potential. In order for me to be happy, I need to be me, not you or someone you want me to be.
- Be an individual and create your own happiness. Then you can teach me the same, and I can live a happy, successful and fulfilling life."

It ends with, "Thank you for hearing me. I love you!"

If only we had all been raised with those ideals. Instead, most of us were raised in the emotional dis-regulation of our parents' unresolved woundedness. Everyday, I try to make it my goal to love with a clarity of intention and with an empathetic presence. Then I do my best to repeat, repeat, repeat. I know that I can't prevent my sons from experiencing life's messiness, but I can cultivate a relationship with them that fosters attunement and safety, even in this messy world.

Cathy recently learned a similar lesson when her son started going through puberty:

> *When Robert's voice changed, he stopped singing. He used to sing around the house, and then I noticed he that he stopped singing at church. I had been encouraging him to come to the choir, and kept telling him about this song we were singing that I knew he loved. A couple of days later, Robert was watching this TV show about a dad pressuring his daughter to run for student council. The father kept saying, "You're just nervous," and I realized that's exactly what I had been doing to Robert. I told him, "That's pretty bad when parents do that to their kids, and I need to try not to do that." He smiled at me, and then I joked, "But you need to come to choir because you're just nervous." We both laughed.*

That is the beauty of healing relationships and the laughter that comes with them. As Cathy said, "I just parent so differently now. I used to see my kids as my appendages, my property really, but now I see my children as people."

"This beautiful, blissful stillness"

Last year, I went on vacation with my children. I will never forget the moment. I was with my two sons, walking along the beach in San Diego, listening to the crashing of the waves, the sounds of the birds, and the gentle chatter of the other beachgoers around us. We walked out onto a rock and looked at the waves. I held both my sons' hands amidst this beautiful, blissful stillness, and all I could think was, "God is so sweet."

My children are adopted and have—and will continue to have—their issues related to that experience. I am grateful to have walked the journey I have and to be able to offer them a safe and sober father they can build a lifelong connection and attachment to.

Through our work, we are all able to be in better relationship with each other and ourselves. Every evening, before I enter my home, I take a moment to let go of work and other pressures in my daily life that would interfere with my connection with my kids.

From our facial expressions, to how we listen, to how we touch one another, we must begin to live in the awareness of how we are communicating with the people we love. It is in our closest relationships that we have the potential to do the greatest harm or to affect the most positive of changes. According to John Gottman in *The Seven Principles for Making Marriage Work*, "Every couple in their daily life together messes up on communications, and every marriage has a dark side: It seems that what matters most is the ability to repair things when they go wrong."

"I knew I belonged there"

There are many roads to healing, but perhaps the most available and least expensive are twelve step programs. For years, twelve steps programs have been offering a process similar to SomEx^SM, but without even realizing it. Through working the twelve steps, people have been changing their brains for over seventy-five years.

Just as somatic experiential therapies ask that we attend, trust, modify our behaviors, regulate our emotional arousal, and then finally enter into deep practice, so the twelve steps have helped people to do just that.

In step one, people admit that they are powerless over addiction and that it has made their lives unmanageable. They are finally attending to the problem at hand. Instead of living in the collapse or arousal of their addictions, they are recognizing the unmanageability of their behaviors.

The second and third steps of "came to believe in a power greater than ourselves," and "became willing to turn our will and our lives over to the care of God," are what trust is all about. In this new space of integrity and faith, people begin to trust and attune to themselves and others, finding that place where they can begin the process of repair.

In the fourth and fifth steps, we "made a searching and fearless moral inventory of ourselves," and "admitted to God, to ourselves, and to another human being the exact nature of our wrongs." Here we are engaged in the process of memory modification, the place where we have the opportunity to tell the story from the right hemisphere. Though twelve step groups do not share in experiential therapy's use of props and role-play (and thank God they don't), they do share in a wonderful display of somatic empathy wherein one addict relates to and helps another.

In the twelve steps, people learn the processes of unlearning and regulation through the sixth, seven, eighth, and ninth steps. This happens by embracing willingness ("Were entirely ready to have God remove all these defects of character"), humility ("Humbly asked God to remove our shortcomings), and action ("Made a list of all persons harmed" and "made direct amends to such people wherever possible").

In the final phase of deep practice, we find steps ten, eleven and twelve, the maintenance steps of all twelve step programs: "continued to take personal inventory," "sought through prayer and mediation to improve our conscious contact with God as we understand Him," and "we tried to carry this message…and practice these principles in all of our affairs."

Together, these steps have become a foundational tool used in many therapeutic approaches. Though they are not the only solution to addiction, science is now proving what those in recovery have long believed: that the intuitive actions and conscious contact of twelve step work ultimately leads to recovery not just from addiction but from the many of our disordered attachments.

I love the twelve steps, but they are not the only solution. There are many paths to peace. Twelve-step fellowship and SomEx^SM are just two of many methods for recovery. As another example, author Sharon Wegscheider-Cruse outlines her own twelve steps for healing:

1. Seek appropriate help.
2. Seek a wise therapist or sponsor.
3. Dedicate yourself to the truth.
4. Become a choice maker.
5. Accept responsibility for yourself.
6. Plan a self-care program.
7. Love wisely.
8. Commit yourself.
9. Claim your personal power.
10. Assess your relationships.
11. Honor aloneness.
12. Open yourself to serendipity.

Before you finish this book, I ask that you sit down and see what steps you need to take to begin creating more emotional harmony in your own life. It's like Sharon says, "Choice making is about choosing healing." And at the end of the day, that is all we are trying to do. We are trying to heal, to transform, to become present in this humming symphony of the world around us. And when we join in that song, we discover the resiliency of our new relationships, and we bring harmony into the old ones. We become a part of the world in a way we never thought possible. Just as I have. Just as Cathy has done. Just as I hope for you.

Bibliography

Adams, Kenneth M. Silently Seduced: When Parents Make Their Children Partners. Deerfield Beach: HCI, 1991.

Arterburn. Addicted to "Love": Understanding Dependencies of the Heart: Romance, Relationship, and Sex. Ann Arbor: Vine Books, 1991.

Berger, Dave and Kathy Kain. "Orienting and Defensive Responses: A Motor Developmental Perspective," presented at International Somatic Experiencing Conference in Berkeley, CA, 2007.

Carnes, Patrick. Facing the Shadow: Starting Sexual and Relationship Recovery. Carefree, AZ: Gentle Path Press, 2001.

Carnes, Patrick J. The Betrayal Bond: Breaking Free of Exploitative Relationships. Deerfield Beach: HCI, 1997.

Carnes, Patrick J. Sexual Anorexia: Overcoming Sexual Self-Hatred. Center City, MN: Hazelden, 1997.

Damasio, Antonio. Looking for Spinoza: Joy, Sorrow, and the Feeling Brain. New York: Houghton Mifflin Harcourt, 2003.

Dayton, Tian. The Drama Within: Psychodrama and Experiential Therapy, Deerfield Beach: Health Communications Inc., 1994.

Dayton, Tian. The Living Stages: A Step-by-Step Guide to Psychodrama, Sociometry and Experiential group Therapy. Deerfield Beach: HCI, 2005.

De Zulueta, Felicity. From Pain to Violence: The Traumatic Roots of Destructiveness. New York: John Wiley & Sons, 2006.

Frankl, Victor. Man's Search for Meaning. Boston: Beacon Press: 1996 (reissue).

Friel, John and Linda. An Adult Child's Guide to What is "Normal." Deerfield Beach, FL: HCI, 1990.

Gottman, John. The Seven Principles for Making Marriage Work: A Practical Guide from the Country's Foremost Relationship Expert. New York: Crown, 1999.

Johnson, Don and Grand, Ian (Ed.). The Body in Psychotherapy: Inquiries in Somatic Psychology. Berkeley, CA: North Atlantic Books, 1998.

Jung, Carl. The Essential Jung. Princeton: Princeton University Press, 2013.

Katehakis, Alexandra. Erotic Intelligence: Igniting Hot, Healthy Sex While in Recovery from Sex Addiction. Deerfield Beach: HCI, 2010.

Koch, Kristof. The Quest for Consciousness: A Neurobiological Approach. Greenwood Village, CO: Roberts & Company, 2004.

Levine, Peter A. Healing Trauma: A Pioneering Program for Restoring the Wisdom of Your Body. Boulder: Sounds true, 2005.

Maltz, Wendy. The Sexual Healing Journey: A Guide for Survivors of Sexual Abuse (Third Ed.). New York: William Morrow Paperbacks, 2012.

Mathew, M. "The body as instrument." Journal of the British Association of Psychotherapists, 35 (1998).

Meares, Russell. The Metaphor of Play: Origin and Breakdown of Personal Being. New York: Routledge, 2005.

Mellody, Pia. Facing Love Addiction: Giving Yourself the Power to Change the Way you Love. San Francisco: Harper Collins San Francisco, 1991.

Nolte, John. The Philosophy, Theory and Methods of J. L. Moreno: The Man Who Tried to Become God. New York: Routledge, 2014.

Panskepp, Jaak. Affective consciousness: Core emotional feelings in animals and humans. Conscious Cognition, Mar 14(1), 2005.

Panskepp, Jaak and Biven, Lucy The Archaeology of the Mind: Neuroevolutionary Origins of Human Emotions. New York: W.W. Norton & Company, 2012.

Porges, Stephen. The Polyvagal Theory: Neurophysiological Foundations of Emotions, Attachment, Communication, and Self-regulation. New York: W.W. Norton & Company, 2011.

Rossi, Ernest. The Psychobiology of Mind-body Healing: New Concepts of Therapeutic Hypnosis. W.W. Norton and Company, 1993.

Schore, A. N. Attachment and the regulation of the right brain. Attachment & Human Development 2 (2000).

Schore, A. N. "Attachment, affect regulation, and the developing right brain: Linking developmental neuroscience to pediatrics." Pediatrics In Review, 26, (2005).

Schore, Allan and Judith. "Modern Attachment Theory: The Central Role of Affect Regulation in Development and Treatment." Clinical Social Work Journal, Volume 36, Issue 1 (March 2008).

Schwarz, Robert. Tools for Transforming Trauma. London: Routledge, 2002.

Siegel, Dan. The Mindful Brain: Reflection and Attunement in the Cultivation of Well-Being. New York: W.W. Norton & Company, 2007.

Siegel, Dan. Mindsight: The New Science of Personal Transformation. New York: Bantam, 2010.

Siegel, Dan and Hartzell, Mary. Parenting from the Inside Out: How a Deeper Self-Understanding Can Help You Raise Children Who Thrive. New York: Tarcher, 2003.

Wegscheider-Cruse, Sharon. Choicemaking: For Spirituality Seekers, Co-Dependents and Adult Children. Deerfield Beach, FL: HCI, 1986.

About the Author

Kent D. Fisher holds a Master's degree in Substance Abuse Counseling from the University of Louisiana, and has over 25 years experience in the field of treating addiction, trauma, codependency, and related disorders. He has a specialization in the area of human sexuality and working with issues of identity, orientation, abuse or addiction, and helping to restore individuals to their healthy sexual/relational selves.

He is the co-founder of the Experiential Healing Center, and co-creator of Somatic Experiential Therapy (SET). He is on the certification board for SET and conducts trainings throughout the country. Kent has previously taught college courses in counseling and psychology. He has trained with pioneers in the field of addiction and mental health such as Patrick Carnes, Claudia Black, and Tian Dayton, as well as worked with the indigenous tribal elders of the Lakota Reservation. He completed a two-year fellowship with Sharon Stanley to become a Certified Somatic Transformation Therapist, is a Certified Sex Addiction Therapist Supervisor. Kent has presented at various conferences and workshops, including the American Counseling Association and the American Psychological Association. He is licensed as an Addiction Specialist and Certified in Experiential Therapy, among other credentials he holds.

Kent lives in Memphis with his two sons, Jamie and Jordan.